CAMBRIDGE   for ESOL

PHOTOCOPIABLE

English at Work

Practical language activities for working in the UK

CAMBRIDGE UNIVERSITY PRESS
Cambridge, New York, Melbourne, Madrid, Cape Town, Singapore,
São Paulo, Delhi, Dubai, Tokyo, Mexico City

Cambridge University Press
The Edinburgh Building, Cambridge CB2 8RU, UK

www.cambridge.org
Information on this title: www.cambridge.org/9780521182546

First published 2011

Printed in the United Kingdom at the University Press, Cambridge

A catalogue record for this publication is available from the British Library

ISBN 978-0-521-18254-6 Paperback

Contents

Map of the book

Theme	Unit	Type of activity	Aim	AECC*
1 Looking for work	1a Your CV	Reading and listening to advice on CV writing	To familiarise learners with the conventions of CV writing.	Rt/E3.7a; Lr/E3.2a; Rt/L1.4a; Lr/L1.2a
	1b Job hunting	Reading about and discussing problems looking for work; matching advice to problems	To develop learners' job-hunting skills.	Rt/E3.4a; Rw/L1.2a; Sd/L1.2b
	1c Get online	Using search results to look for jobs	To develop learners' online jobseeking skills.	Rt/E3.3a; Rt/L1.3a
2 Applying for work	2a The language of recruitment	Reading an article about the jargon of job advertisements	To familiarise learners with jargon related to recruitment.	Rt/E3.1a; Rt/L1.1a
	2b Job adverts	Reading and discussing job adverts; listening and noticing job-related vocabulary	To develop learners' ability to understand job adverts.	Rt/E3.7a; Sd/E3.1d; Rt/L1.5a; Sd/L1.2a
	2c Applying in writing for a job	Applying guidelines for writing job applications	To develop learners' ability to compose coherent text and write a successful job application letter.	Wt/E3.1a; Wt/L1.3a
3 Job interviews	3a Interview tips	Exchange of advice for job interviews	To raise awareness of how to prepare before and how to behave during a job interview.	Lr/E3.5b; Rt/E3.8a; Rt/L1.5a; Lr/L1.3a
	3b At the interview	Reading and listening to different answers to the same interview questions; discussing effective (and ineffective) responses	To familiarise learners with good interview technique.	Lr/E3.6a; Sc/E3.4a; Lr/L1.6b; Sc/L1.3b
	3c After the interview	Listening to a dialogue; making inferences	To develop learners' listening skills; to encourage learners to see their performance at job interviews from the perspective of an interviewer.	Lr/E3.7b; Rw/L1.2a; Lr/L1.6b
4 Your new job	4a Chatting with colleagues	Listening to different versions of conversations to identify polite strategies	To give learners practice in making accurate and appropriate contributions to social interactions in the workplace.	Lr/E3.6a; Sd/E3.1a; Lr/L1.6d; Sd/L1.1a
	4b Modern job titles	Reading and discussing a blog	To raise students' awareness of different job titles.	Rw/E3.3a; Rt/E3.2a; Rw/L1.1a; Rt/L1.2a
	4c Company structure	Describing company structure	To familiarise learners with the terminology for talking about relationships between different departments and levels in an organisation.	Rt/E3.8a; Rt/E3.9a; Rt/L1.4a; Sc/L1.2b
5 Terms and conditions	5a Agency work	Reading a webpage; writing an email	To develop learners' reading skills.	Rt/E3.6a; Rt/E3.7a; Rt/L1.5b
	5b Company policies	Reading a webpage and listening to a phone conversation	To develop learners' ability to listen to and understand explanations.	Lr/E3.1c; Sc/E3.3c; Lr/L1.6b; Sc/L1.2b
	5c Understanding an employment contract	Matching definitions and reading an employment contract	To develop learners' ability to read and understand official language used in contracts and other workplace documents.	Rw/E3.5a; Rt/L1.2a

*AECC = Adult ESOL Core Curriculum

Theme	Unit	Type of activity	Aim	AECC*
6 Health and safety	6a Danger! Understanding health and safety signs	Reading, understanding and discussing common health and safety signs in the workplace	To familiarise students with common health and safety signs.	Rt/E3.9a; Rt/L1.3a
	6b Health and safety training	Listening to a health and safety briefing	To provide practice in listening to a training presentation.	Lr/E3.2a; Lr/L1.2a
	6c Reporting accidents	Reading and writing a report about a workplace accident	To develop students' ability to plan and write a report in paragraphs.	Rt/E3.1a; Wt/E3.2a; Rt/L1.1a; Wt/L1.1; Wt/L1.3a
7 Computers at work	7a Computer language	Matching definitions to computing lexis	To develop learners' vocabulary.	Rw/E3.1a; Rw/L1.2a
	7b Computer maintenance	Reading a webpage about computer problems	To develop learners' gist and detail reading skills.	Rt/E3.3a; Rt/L1.4a; Ws/E3.1a; Ws/L1.2a
	7c IT helpdesk	Listening to a phone call between colleagues; role play of phone conversation.	To develop learners' ability to ask for and give help on the phone.	Lr/E3.2b; Sc/E3.3c; Lr/L1.2a; Sc/L1.3d
8 Equal opportunities	8a Case studies	Discussion of disputes between employee and employer	To develop learners' skills in listening to each other.	Rt/E3.4a; Rt/L1.5a; Sd/E3.1d; Sd/L1.2a
	8b Disability Discrimination Act	Listening to a conversation about training and answering multiple choice questions.	To develop students' listening skills and raise awareness of the Disability Discrimination Act (DDA).	Lr/E3.7b; Lr/E3.6a; Lr/L1.1a
	8c Equal opportunities monitoring	Listening to a discussion and completing a form	To provide practice filling in a form; to raise awareness of concerns and priorities of an equal opportunities employer.	Lr/E3.3a; Lr/E3.6a; Lr/L1.1a
9 Money	9a Talking big money	Reading and matching definitions	To develop learners' practical knowledge and vocabulary relating to work and pay in the UK.	Rw/E3.1a; Rw/E3.2a; Rw/L1.2a
	9b Getting paid	Listening and correcting details on a pay claim form	To develop learners' listening, numeracy and form-filling skills.	Lr/E3.2b; Rw/E3.2a; Wt/E3.5a; Lr/1.1a; Wt/L1.6a
	9c Payment queries	Reading online postings and their responses	To develop learners' ability to read websites for specific information.	Rt/E3.4a; Wt/E3.2a; Rt/L1.5a; Wt/L1.5a
10 Dealing with problems	10a Phoning in sick	Listening to a phone call in which an employee phones in sick. Practising the conversation	To demonstrate common practice for reporting absence through sickness in the UK; to raise awareness of appropriate language for discussing health issues sensitively.	Lr/E3.1c; Sc/E3.4d; Lr/L1.2a; Sc/L1.3d
	10b Dealing with customer complaints	Listening to phone messages; reading and analysing emails; writing an email	To develop students' listening, note-taking and email writing skills.	Lr/E3.3b; Ww/E3.1a; Lr/L1.1a; Wt/L1.4a
	10c Everyday problems	Reading a blog and focussing on problem-related vocabulary	To present problem-related vocabulary in context, and encourage learners to use context to work out meaning.	Rw/E3.5a; Rt/E3.4a; Rt/L1.5a; Rw/L1.3a

*AECC = Adult ESOL Core Curriculum

Map of the book

Theme	Unit	Type of activity	Aim	AECC*
11 Employee rights	11a What's the law?	Discussion; listening to radio interview	To develop learners' speaking and listening skills.	Lr/E3.2a; Rw/E3.1a; Lr/1.2a
	11b Annual leave	Roleplay negotiation about leave times	To give learners practice at taking part in a spoken negotiation.	Sd/E3.1f; Sd/E3.1g; Sd/L1.3a; Lr/L1.2b;
	11c Maternity and paternity leave	Reading and discussing an information text	To develop learners' reading skills, vocabulary and knowledge of UK workplace practices.	Sd/E3.1d; Rt/E3.4a; Sd/L1.2a; Rt/L1.5a;
12 The work environment	12a Helping out	Listening to dialogues	To familiarise learners with a range of strategies for dealing politely and helpfully with members of the public.	Lr/3.1c; Lr/E3.7d; Lr/L1.1a; Lr/L1.6d
	12b A green workplace	Reading a web article; listening to two colleagues discussing the article; discussion	To develop learners' reading, listening and speaking skills.	Rt/E3.7a; Lr/E3.1b; Lr/L1.6a; Rt/L1.5a
	12c Working outdoors	Reading an article; matching headings to paragraphs	To develop learners' ability to determine text purpose; to give practice in reading for detail.	Rt/E3.4a; Rw/E3.5a; Rt/L1.5a; Rw/L1.2a
13 Qualifications	13a Qualifications in the UK	Reading a blog; matching questions and answers	To develop learner's reading skills and knowledge of UK qualifications.	Rt/E3.4a; Rt/L1.5a
	13b Exam task practice	Discussing exam tips; practising reading and listening exam tasks	To develop learners' reading and listening skills in some of the task types common in exams.	Rt/E3.4a; Lr/E3.2a; Rt/L1.5a; Lr/L1.2a
	13c Evaluating a student's exam performance	Reading, listening to and evaluating a learner's performance in writing and speaking exam tasks	To develop learners' awareness of what constitutes effective performance in exams.	Lr/E3.1c; Lr/L1.6a; Sd/L1.1b; Wt/L1.3a
14 Customer service	14a Telephoning	Listening to telephone conversations	To develop learners' ability to talk effectively and politely on the phone.	Sd/E3.1f; Sd/E3.1b; Sd/L1.2c; Sd/L1.1b
	14b Service with a smile	Listening to service encounters	To raise learners' awareness of what sounds polite.	Sc/E3.1a; Sc/E3.3a; Sc/L1.1a; Lr/L1.2b
	14c Customer service Snakes and Ladders	Role playing service encounters; playing a board game	To provide learners with practice at polite interaction with members of the public in a work context.	Sd/E3.1b; Sc/E3.4d; Sc/L1.1b
15 Communication	15a Email or snail mail?	Sorting vocabulary items	To develop learners' vocabulary related to email; raise awareness of email etiquette.	Rw/E3.3a; Rw/L1.1a; Wt/L1.4a
	15b Getting it right	Multiple choice quiz; correcting a letter	To provide accuracy practice.	Sc/E3.4a; Sc/L1.3a Ws/L1.3a
	15c Checking details	Checking and correcting details about future plans	To give learners practice at clarifying arrangements including times, addresses, prices, costs and email addresses.	Sd/E3.1f; Sd/E3.2b; Sd/L1.4a
16 A new start	16a Moving on	Comparing different emails connected with leaving a job	To develop learners' awareness of appropriate register and develop writing skills.	Rt/E3.1a; Wt/E3.2a; Rt/L1.1a; Wt/L1.3a
	16b Entrepreneurs	Jigsaw reading about business start-ups	To develop reading and speaking skills.	Rt/E3.4a; Sc/E3.4c; Rt/L1.5a; Sc/L1.3b
	16c Business start-up	Roleplay negotiation	To develop speaking and negotiation skills.	Sd/E3.1b; Lr/E3.5b; Sd/L1.1b; Lr/L1.2b

*AECC = Adult ESOL Core Curriculum

Thanks and acknowledgements

Author's thanks

With thanks to Frances Disken and all at Cambridge University Press for their help in preparing this material for publication. And finally, thank you, Bellamy, for arranging a successful move.

Publisher's acknowledgements

The author and publishers would like to thank the following individuals who reviewed the draft material during development: Ken Milgate, Anna Pemberton and Nida Ryall.

The author and publishers acknowledge the following sources of copyright material and are grateful for the permissions granted. While every effort has been made, it has not always been possible to identify the sources of all the material used, or to trace all copyright holders. If any omissions are brought to our notice, we will be happy to include the appropriate acknowledgements on reprinting.

p. 17: Paul Mackenzie-Cummins writing for monster.co.uk for the adapted text 'Recruitment industry insider Paul Mackenzie-Cummins explains what job ads really mean'. Reproduced with kind permission; p. 79: Shirley Siluk Gregory for the adapted text 'Green living, green working?' © Shirley Siluk Gregory. Shirley Siluk Gregory is a writer/analyst who covers environmental and sustainability issues; p. 81: Danny Chadburn writing for monster.co.uk for the adapted text 'A Change of scene' from 'Working outdoors'; p. 103, text 1: Phil Cavalier-Lumley. Reproduced with kind permission; p. 103, text 2: Bobby Patel. Reproduced with kind permission; p. 103, text 3: Sarah Thomas. Reproduced with kind permission.

The publishers are grateful to the following for permission to reproduce copyright photographs and material:
Key: l = left, c = centre, r = right, t = top, b = bottom
Alamy/©Art Directors & Trip for p. 11, /©Keith Morris for p. 27(tr), /©Big Cheese Photo LLC for p. 37(t), /©Moodboard for p. 37(l), /©Fancy for p. 37(r), /©Radius Images for p. 55(tr), /©Allesalltag for p. 65(b), /©Alterstock for p. 65(t), /©Bubbles for p. 77(lc), /©MBI for p. 77(r), /©Marc Macdonald for p. 77(rc), /©Shout for p. 77(tl); Corbis/©Asia Images for p. 27(tl), /©Strauss Curtis for p. 27(tc), /©Image Source for p. 55(l), /©Larry Williams for p. 55(b); Shutterstock/©Shutterstock for p. 31, /© RT Images for p. 45, /©Michael Jung for p. 61; Phil Cavalier-Lumley for p. 103(t), Bobby Patel for p. 103(c), Sarah Thomas for p. 103(b).

Audio recording: Ian Harker
Picture research: Alison Prior
Illustrations: Laura Martinez, Ben Swift and Ian West

Introduction

Who is *English at Work* for?

English at Work is for teachers and learners of ESOL and EFL in colleges and schools, as well as in workplace settings. It is designed primarily for learners who are in work, or are seeking work in the UK; it is also suitable for learners who are planning to move to the UK for work. It is aimed at intermediate to upper intermediate learners (National Qualifications Framework: Entry 3 to Level 1; Common European Framework: B1 to B2).

The activities are self-contained lessons for the busy teacher who wants material which will help their learners use English in their workplaces. The activities are mutually independent, and can be used in any order, depending on the needs of the learners.

English at Work is designed to be used in both general English classes and ESOL for Work exam preparation classes. Theme 13 contains exam practice tasks for exam candidates. However, teachers are advised to refer to the websites of the relevant exam board for further information about the ESOL for Work exams they offer, and for further practice material.

How is *English at Work* organised?

There are 16 themes connected with the world of work, such as Health and safety (theme 6), Employee rights (theme 11) and Customer service (theme 14). Themes 1–3 deal with looking for work, applying for work and job interviews, while theme 16 addresses the aspirations of learners who may wish to start a business of their own.

Each theme consists of three units. The contexts in the units are intended to be representative of the kinds of work learners are engaged in. These contexts include a catering company (5b), a hotel (6b), a warehouse (10a), an office (12b), a hairdresser's (14a) and many others. However, in each case the content and vocabulary are designed to be relevant to all learners, whatever their job. Most units feature the contextualised presentation and practice of work-related vocabulary, and most integrate two or more skills. The main focus is on speaking, listening and reading, as these are the skills most likely to be of use to learners in the workplace. Some writing practice is included, and this is always based around a text type that is likely to be of use in learners' working lives, such as a CV (1a), a pay claim form (9b) or an apologetic email to a customer (10b).

The map of the book provides a clear overview of the 48 units, including AECC references and lesson aims in order to help the teacher select appropriate units to support their course.

How is each unit organised?

Each unit consists of two pages: Teacher's notes on the left-hand page and a photocopiable worksheet on the right-hand page, providing approximately 40–50 minutes of teaching time. There are also self-study exercises for each unit, which can be given as homework. These can be found in the back of the book, while the answers to the exercises are at the bottom of the corresponding Teacher's notes page.

At the top of the Teacher's notes, the shaded information panel contains the following information:

Type of activity: A summary of the language skills practised and their relevance to life at work, as well as suggested groupings.

AECC references: The Adult ESOL Core Curriculum descriptors demonstrating achievement at Entry 3 and Level 1.

Aims: The rationale for the activity; students' learning goals with reference to how the activities should enable them to cope with workplace situations.

Vocabulary: Lexis which learners need to know to complete the tasks. You may wish to pre-teach this. Note: the self-study activities provide further practice of using much of this lexis.

Preparation: This outlines what the teacher will need to do before the lesson in order to use the materials. This includes what to photocopy, any activity cards which need cutting up, extra things to bring to the lesson and any pre-lesson reading which would be useful for the teacher.

Differentiation: A range of suggested strategies to accommodate learner differences within the same group. This section offers guidance on the grouping of learners and/or ways to adapt the task to meet the diverse range of student needs. More on differentiation is provided below under 'What is the best way to use *English at Work* in the classroom?'

Each unit is divided into three stages – a *Warmer* to get the learners thinking about the subject and to demonstrate to the teacher how much they know of the subject and its related vocabulary; the *Main activities* on the worksheet, which are supported with step by step instructions and answers on the teacher's notes; an *Extension* activity, to help teachers review and develop the learning that has taken place. These range from the learners conducting web-based research about pay and taxation (9c) to noticing, and reporting back on their noticing of colloquial language outside the classroom (12a).

Some topics recur throughout the book, such as employment law, which provides the context for units 5a, 8a and 11a, b and c. In cases such as these, the link is cross-referenced at the bottom of the teacher's notes under *Links to other themes in this book*. This is to enable teachers to identify related activities which might be of use to their learners.

The worksheets themselves are photocopiable; some require cutting up for the classroom activity, and all are suitable as handouts for the students. Many of the activities have accompanying audio material, which features a range of native and non-native speaker accents. For some of the tasks, the teacher is advised to refer the students to the language in the audioscript, which is also photocopiable.

What is the best way to use *English at Work* in the classroom?

The Map of the book highlights the 16 themes and 48 units. Teachers can refer to this map to choose the most suitable themes or individual units for the needs of their particular learners.

For each unit, differentiation strategies are suggested in order for the material to be presented in a way that best meets the wide-ranging needs of learners. In many cases, this is a suggestion of how to adapt the material for stronger and weaker learners in the same class. However, many other differentiation strategies are also presented: for example units 7a and 15a propose ways in which a teacher could differentiate according to the differing levels of IT proficiency of their students. Recognising that learners react differently to different approaches in the classroom, alternatives are presented for learners with a kinaesthetic learning style (16a). Teachers may also feel it is appropriate to differentiate by learners' experience, whether of looking for work (1), becoming parents (11c) or dealing with banks (16c).

How will *English at Work* help my students?

The activities are aimed at all learners regardless of what work they do or are looking for. The content is intended to be generic, rather than to aim at specific learners in specific trades. Unit 6c, for example, uses a scenario of a minor accident at a construction site to develop learners' report writing skills. But the skills development in this unit is as relevant to learners working in other sectors as it would be to construction workers themselves. Likewise, the vocabulary presented is intended to be universally applicable, and specialist terms which would not be of use to many learners are avoided.

The materials offer vocabulary-learning opportunities, and the skills focus is primarily on speaking, listening and reading.

What preparation will I need to do before each class?

The Teacher's notes make clear what preparation is required – where it would be useful for the teacher or learners to refer to websites, this is clearly stated.

1a Your CV

Type of activity
Reading and listening to advice on CV writing. Individual and pair work.

AECC reference
Rt/E3.7a; Lr/E3.2a; Rt/L1.4a; Lr/L1.2a

Aims
To familiarise learners with the conventions of CV writing.

Vocabulary
make sb tick, specific, update, concise, get rid of, lose, vague

Preparation
Photocopy one worksheet for each learner.

Differentiation
Learners with little or no experience of writing a CV could be shown example CVs at the beginning of the class, and can be grouped with learners who have written a CV for task 1.

Warmer
Elicit from the learners what a CV is for, what information is included on a CV, and how many of them have written a CV in English or their own language already.

1 Give each learner a worksheet. Ask them to check which of the sections of a CV they mentioned in the warmer. Ask them to read the advice quickly to match the paragraphs with the section headings. Ask learners to check their answers in pairs.

> **Answers**
> **a** Interests and Achievements
> **b** Employment history
> **c** Personal profile
> **d** Personal details
> **e** Education and Qualifications
> **f** Additional information
> **g** References

2 Ask learners to look at Orhan's CV and answer the question in pairs.

> **Answers**
> Personal profile; Personal details; Education and qualifications; Interests; Additional information; References. *Employment history* is missing because Orhan has not yet worked.

3 Discuss this question as a whole class, but do not give feedback until after task 4.

4 (▶2) Explain that learners are going to listen to a conversation between Orhan and Julian, a careers advisor at his college. Ask learners to listen for any suggestions that Julian makes that are the same as their own. Play the recording and conduct feedback. If you are working in an institution where there is somebody with a similar role, ask if the learners know what the person's name is, where they work, what they do and how learners could make an appointment.

5 (▶2) Give learners time to read the question (make sure they understand the word *specific*), and then play the recording again. Ask learners to check their answers with a partner.

> **Answers**
> a ✓ b ✗ c ✗ d ✗ e ✓ f ✓ g ✗ h ✓

6 Put learners in pairs to do this task. Conduct feedback by asking pairs to share their lists with the rest of the class.

Extension
Learners bring in or type a CV, bearing in mind the suggestions from the website in task 2 and Julian's comments in task 5, and submit to their teacher for comments and suggestions. If possible, learners could also make an appointment with a careers advisor at their college or local job centre to discuss their CV.

Links to other themes in this book
For more on looking for work and applying for jobs, see 2 and 3.

Answers: Self-study exercises

1 1 a 2 a 3 a 4 b 5 b

2 1 No way! 2 take a seat 3 a long story
  4 to be honest 5 fair enough

1 Look at the tips from a recruitment website about writing a CV. Write the section headings in the right place.

> Additional information   Personal profile   References   Employment history
> Interests and Achievements   Education and Qualifications   Personal details

Super CV

a _____

Some people don't bother with this at all, but remember the person reading your CV wants to have some idea about what makes you tick. Avoid general things though, like 'Reading' or 'Watching films', and try and include things that are interesting and/or relevant to the job.

b _____

If you've been working for some time, this should go before the details about your education. Start with what you're doing now, and work backwards.

c _____

This part is just to summarise your skills, work achievements and career aims. It only needs to be a few lines – you can provide more details later on.

d _____

This section needs little more than your name and contact details. People often include nationality, marital status and age, but to be honest, recruiters can usually make a decision without this information.

e _____

Start with the most recent, and work backwards. And remember to be precise – it should be clear exactly

which school or college you attended, even if it was in another country.

f _____

Anything can go in here – so long as it's relevant and doesn't fit better in a different section. For example, you could say that you have a clean driving licence, or explain any breaks in your CV.

g _____

At least one of these people should be work related, like a past or current line manager. You don't need to include their names on the CV though – you could just write 'Available on request'.

2 Complete Orhan's CV with section headings from task 1. Which one is missing?

ORHAN KARACA: CV

A bilingual man (English and Turkish), about to finish college, seeking a challenging position that offers professional growth

Name	Orhan Karaca
Email	orhan1990@homemail.co.uk
DOB	21/9/1990

2009	Grindleford College: studying A levels in ICT and Maths
2004–07	Grindleford College. 5 GCSEs inc. Maths
1997–2004	Gaziantep School, Gaziantep, Turkey

• organised a school raffle which raised £410 for charity
• football

• clean driving licence
• willing to work shifts and weekends

Ms Nasima Sarwar, ICT teacher, Grindleford College.
N.sarwar@grindleford.ac.uk

3 Can you suggest any changes Orhan should make to his CV?

4 Listen to Julian, a careers advisor, give Orhan advice about his CV. Were any of Julian's suggestions the same as yours?

5 Put a tick (✓) next to the advice Julian gives Orhan.

a regularly make changes to his CV
b make his CV longer
c correct the mistakes in his CV
d add a different photo
e remove his date of birth
f be more specific
g add his National Insurance number
h include what he did between 2007 and 2009

6 Work with a partner. Make a list of CV dos and don'ts.

1b Job hunting

Type of activity
Reading about and discussing problems looking for work; matching advice to problems. Individual, pair and group work.

AECC reference
Rt/E3.4a; Rw/L1.2a; Sd/L1.2b

Aims
To develop learners' job-hunting skills.

Vocabulary
rob, stuck, covering letter, candidate, applicant, feel cheated, mislead, dull, reject, rejection, speculative application

Preparation
Photocopy one worksheet for each learner.

Differentiation
Kinaesthetic learners: for a more kinaesthetic approach, you could copy the postings (1–4) and the responses (A–D) onto coloured cards, and cut them up for a matching activity.

Warmer
Elicit from the learners how they feel about looking for work (answers are likely to be rather negative), and problems people may experience while looking for work. (Possible answers: loss of motivation, depression, uncertainty.) Explain that they are going to look at an article which deals with some of these negative experiences, and gives advice.

1 Give each learner a worksheet. Ask learners to discuss the question in pairs. Conduct feedback.

2 Ask learners to read the full postings and match them to the titles in task 1.

> **Answers**
> 1 All that effort, but still no luck
> 2 Stuck for ideas
> 3 I feel like I've been robbed
> 4 Still looking for that dream job

3 Put learners in small groups and ask them to discuss what they think each person should do. Allow some time for discussions and then give one set of response cards to each group. Ask each group to match the responses to the postings. Check answers, and ask learners which replies were similar to their own suggestions, and which are most helpful.

> **Answers**
> **1**A **2**D **3**B **4**C

Extension
The texts contain some useful vocabulary which you may wish to teach your learners: *covering letter, writer's block, applicant, vacancies, letter of rejection, candidate, proactive, speculative applications, collaborating.*

Links to other themes in this book
For more on looking for work and applying for jobs, see 2 and 3.

> **Answers: Self-study exercises**
>
> **1** 1 for 2 off 3 with 4 in 5 through
> **2** 1 b 2 d 3 e 4 a 5 c

Job hunting 1b

1 Look at the statements posted on an internet forum for jobseekers. What do you think they want advice about?

> I feel like I've been robbed   All that effort, but still no luck
> Still looking for that dream job   Stuck for ideas

2 Now look at the full postings (1-4), and match them to the statements in task 1.

1 I've written a covering letter which I think works pretty well for just about any job I might want to apply for. It's a good letter, and I've sent over 100 copies off (along with my CV) in response to ads I've seen. And how many replies do you think I've had? You guessed it – none!
Dina, Bracknell

2 I've been told I need to add 'Personal profile' onto my CV, but I'm not sure what to write. I keep getting writer's block. Everybody seems to write the same old rubbish. 'Good communicator'? Heard that one before. 'Hard worker'? Everyone says that!
Samantha, London

3 OK, so get this. Had an interview last week for a job I know I should have got. I could tell they liked me – they even said during the interview that I would fit in well. Then got a call today, saying that although they felt I was a strong candidate, they've offered the job to another applicant. I feel angry and cheated. So angry, in fact, that I'm tempted to write and say that they misled me by making me think I'd already got the job.
Jan, Humberside

4 I go through the job pages of my local paper every day, and I've applied for a few jobs, but to be honest, I haven't found anything that really grabs my attention. They all look – well, a bit dull. I've tried my local Job Centre too, but it's the same old story. Any tips?
Moonfish, Norfolk

3 Your teacher will give you some cards with responses to the postings. Match each response to a posting from task 2.

Cards for task 3

A Do not send the same application to multiple jobs. Read the advertisement carefully and adapt your application for it. No two vacancies are identical, and neither should any of your application letters be. If you're just sending mass mailings, it'll probably be obvious. Remember – they're looking for a reason to reject your application. And you've just given them one. **Seeta**

B HOLD IT! Like you, I had a great interview recently, but then got a letter of rejection. So I wrote and thanked them for the opportunity, and said I hoped I'd find another employer like them soon. And then – guess what! The selected candidate changed her mind. They remembered my nice letter, and offered me the job! So, if you write to them, choose your words carefully. You may still be in with a chance. **Robert**

C You're waiting for your dream job to come looking for you. Well, that's not going to happen, as you now know. You're going to have to be more proactive, and broaden your search. Try agencies, look regularly at company websites. And there's nothing wrong with trying a few speculative applications – some vacancies are filled without ever being advertised. **Andrea**

D Hi. I'm a recruiter myself, and the main mistake people make isn't including these over-used phrases. It's failing to provide examples. So instead of saying 'I am a good team player', put 'I am a good team player, because in my work in reception, working with colleagues to solve problems is a must'. You need to support what you say with real-life examples. **Sandra**

1c Get online

Type of activity
Using search results to look for jobs. Individual and group work.

AECC reference
Rt/E3.3a; Rt/L1.3a

Aims
To develop learners' online jobseeking skills and familiarise learners with using the Internet.

Vocabulary
search engine, vacancy, HGV, recruitment, speculative enquiry

Preparation
Photocopy one worksheet for each learner.

Differentiation
IT literacy: group learners who are not IT literate with those who are.

Learners looking for work: if you feel it is appropriate and you have some learners in the group who are looking for work, the role of the other students should be to help the jobseekers find suitable vacancies to apply for.

Warmer
Ask learners if they have ever used a search engine to look for work, and how helpful it was. Explain that they are going to learn about and practise using a search engine to find job vacancies in their area.

1 Give each learner a worksheet. Ask them to work in pairs to answer the questions.

(If you have access to the Internet and a data projector in your classroom, do your own live search.).

Answers
job Bristol; 22,900,000

2 Ask learners to read the results and work in pairs to answer the questions.

Answers
A job waiter **B** bar job Bristol
Search B is more useful because it specifies 'Bristol'.

3 Ask learners to discuss the advice in small groups.

Answers
a ✓ b ✗ c ✓ d ✓

4 Ask learners to work in pairs to do this task.

Answers
All, except *About us* and *Contact us*

Ask learners to discuss what information they would find on the pages *About us* and *Contact us*.

Answers
About us: this page will give a summary of what the company does so is useful for an applicant to see if they would like to work for the company.

Contact us: will give contact details. This is useful if an applicant wants to make a speculative application

5 Explain that when we approach a company who are not advertising jobs, we call this a speculative enquiry. Ask the learners to arrange Moshe's email in the correct order. Elicit whether the students think it is a good idea to send emails like this, and whether they would send one themselves.

Answers
c b i f a h e g d

Extension
Learners use a search engine to find the name of an agency which fills vacancies in your town.

Links to other themes in this book
For more on looking for work and applying for jobs, see 2 and 3.

Answers: Self-study exercises

1 1 ~~search computer~~   search engine   search results
   2 current vacancies   ~~vacant vacancies~~
     job vacancies
   3 ~~speculative job~~   speculative application
     speculative enquiry
   4 job application   ~~job employment~~   job title

2 1 speculative application
   2 job title
   3 search engine
   4 search results

Darren lives in Bristol and has decided to use a search engine to look for vacancies.

1 What has he searched for? How many results did he get?

Google	job Bristol	Search Advanced Search

Web ⊞ Show options...   Results 1 - 10 of about **22,900,000** for **job** Bristol. (0.28 seconds)

This is Bristol Jobs - The Job Search in the Bristol area
Looking for **jobs** in the **Bristol**? At This is **Bristol Jobs**, you can search the **jobs** we currently
have live online. So come & find a **job** at This is **Bristol** ...
jobs.thisisbristol.co.uk/ - Cached - Similar

Sponsored Links
Jobs in Bristol
100s of jobs in Bristol
Admin,Office,Sales,HR,Call Centre

2 Now look at two more searches Darren made. What did he search for? Which search was the most useful?

A

How to get a job as a waiter without experience   results 1-5 of about 3,630,000
Waiting tables can be a fun and lucrative profession. But how do you get a **job** without
experience? This article shows you how.
www.essortment.com/career/getjobwaiterw_sjla.htm - Cached - Similar

B

results 1-5 of about 208,000
Bar jobs in Bristol
Bristol bar **jobs** / **waiter jobs** (463 ads posted). Shortcut to my saved adsListing ... Calling
The Best Bartenders & **Waiters** In **Bristol**. bristol | Permanent ...
bristol.gumtree.com/**bristol**/bar-catering-**jobs**_763_1.html - Cached - Similar

⊞ Show more results from bristol.gumtree.com

3 Tick (✓) the good pieces of advice about using a search engine.

a always write the name of the town or region you want to work in.
b remember to use the word 'in'; e.g. *accounting vacancies in London.*
c try writing different phrases and doing repeat searches: e.g.
   lorry driver Birmingham
   Birmingham vacancy lorry driver
   HGV job Birmingham
   West Midlands lorry job
d check that the site you have found features jobs in the UK, not other parts of the English-speaking
   world (Kenya, Canada, India etc).

4 Another way to find job vacancies is to look at the website of a company you would like to work for. Which of the following could be the title of a job vacancies page on a company website?

Current vacancies   Work with us   About us   Careers   Employment   Recruitment   Jobs   Contact us

5 Put this speculative enquiry in the right order.

a give me the contact details of the person I would need
b I am interested in applying for work with
c Dear Sir or Madam,
d Moshe Green
e forward to hearing from you.
f in sales. I would be very grateful if you could
g With thanks and best wishes,
h to contact to find out about possible opportunities. I look
i Hotphone, and have four years' experience working

2a The language of recruitment

Type of activity
Reading an article about the jargon of job advertisements. Individual and pair work.

AECC reference
Rt/E3.1a; Rt/L1.1a

Aims
To familiarise learners with jargon related to recruitment.

Vocabulary
stock phrase, candidate, recruiter, cliché, recluse, social skills, innovative, salary range, peformance-related pay, equvialent, deadline

Preparation
Photocopy one worksheet for each learner.

Differentiation
Weaker learners: pre-teach the key vocabulary if you think learners will have difficulty working out meaning from context.

Learners with or without work experience: pair up learners who have worked with those who haven't, to encourage peer teaching.

Warmer
Show the learners a local newspaper page of job adverts. Ask if they have ever found job ads unclear or hard to understand. Explain that job advert writers often reuse the same phrases in many different adverts, expecting that all readers will understand them. The aim of the activity is to help them understand the jargon used in job ads.

1 Ask the learners to read the first two paragraphs and decide what the purpose of the text is. Set a time limit for this (e.g. 30 seconds).

> **Answers**
> b

2 Refer learners to the phrases in the boxes and ask them to complete this task in pairs.

> **Answers**
> **1** Team player
> **2** Fixed term
> **3** Dynamic
> **4** Flexible
> **5** Competitive salary
> **6** OTE
> **7** Pro rata
> **8** Closing date

3 Ask learners to re-read the introductory paragraphs and then discuss in pairs which opinions are expressed. Encourage them to say which phrase gave them the answers.

> **Answers**
> **a** N (*being replaced by skilfully written adverts*)
> **b** Y (*does not really tell candidates what the recruiter is actually looking for*)
> **c** N (*most job seekers want straightforward job adverts*)

4 Ask learners to work alone and re-read the definition paragraphs and complete this task. Ask them to check answers in pairs.

> **Answers**
> **a** 3 **b** 7 **c** 8 **d** 1 **e** 5 **f** 2 **g** 4 **h** 6

5 Ask learners to work in small groups to discuss which phrases from task 2 would encourage them to apply for a job, and which would put them off.

Extension
Learners visit the website of a local recruitment agent, print off a job vacancy advert, and look to see if any of the phrases from task 2 are included. Ask if they can find any other phrases whose meaning they do not know.

Links to other themes in this book
For more on looking and applying for work, see 1 and 3.

> **Answers: Self-study exercises**
>
> **1** maternity cover   stock phrases   closing date   performance-related pay   salary range
>
> **2** 1 stock phrases
> 2 maternity cover
> 3 performance-related pay
> 4 closing date
> 5 salary range

The language of recruitment (2a)

1 Read the first two paragraph of the text. What is its purpose?

a to help employers explain their job vacancies more accurately
b to help people understand job adverts more easily
c to warn people about misleading job adverts

○ ✛ ▦ ▾ ⬚ ⬚ ⬚ | 🏠 ▾ 🔊 🖨 ▾ 🗔 Page ▾ ⚙ Tools ▾ »

Recruitment industry insider Paul Mackenzie-Cummins explains what job ads really mean

In today's competitive job marketplace, employers are constantly competing with one another to attract the most suitably qualified candidates. The unimaginative recruitment adverts of yesterday are being replaced by skilfully written adverts designed to lure you. Writing job adverts is now a job in itself.

However, with advertising costs at a premium and ad space restricted, recruiters have to rely on certain characteristics and features that are common to most, if not all, recruitment adverts. The reliance on stock phrases such as 'enthusiastic, dynamic, forward-thinking, proactive team player' does not really tell candidates what the recruiter is actually looking for. Although most job seekers want straightforward job adverts, the clichés are here to stay. So, what do these phrases actually mean?

1 .... As it's unlikely that anyone would claim the opposite, phrases like this become meaningless. When was the last time you saw an advert asking for a 'Recluse with no social skills'?! They essentially want someone with a bit of personality who will fit well into a group.

2 .... Here's one to look out for. This means that the job is only for a limited period, and then you're out. An example would be when there's a vacancy for maternity cover; when the woman returns to work, your contract is over.

3 .... In other words, are you innovative and creative? Although this was often used to replace 'young' after age discrimination legislation was introduced, this can mean anyone with enthusiasm, whatever their age.

4 .... You need to be prepared to meet the demands of the business. But be aware that this could involve relocating, or working shifts, including nights and weekends.

5 .... Why do firms use phrases like this, or 'attractive package'? You wouldn't ask for a test drive of a new car if you didn't know how much it cost to buy first. Try and find out as early in the process as possible what the possible salary range is.

6 .... This means that the salary advertised is partly based on performance-related pay. So you'll need to meet certain targets to earn the full amount. Ask at the interview about the targets and then decide if they are achievable or not. Oh, and by the way, it stands for 'On Target Earnings'.

7 .... You'll see this when the job is part-time. It is usually written next to an equivalent full-time annual salary. So if the salary is £16,000 for a 40-hour week and the vacancy is 20 hours, the pay is £8,000. Don't forget to do the calculation!

8 .... Simple, this is just the deadline for applying. You'd be surprised how many applications are submitted too late. And they just end up in the bin, so don't make the same mistake!

---

2 Below are the eight terms explained in the text, Put them in the right place (1–8) in the text.

Pro rata	Closing date	OTE	Competitive salary	Fixed term	Flexible	Dynamic	Team player

3 Which of the following opinions are expressed in the introduction?

a Job adverts were better written in the past than they are now.
b A lot of job adverts do not make it clear what skills the employer is looking for.
c Recruiters are producing the kind of job adverts that candidates want.

4 In which paragraph (1–8) are the following opinions expressed?

a Some words are used now because of changes in the law.
b Make sure you work out what proportion of a full-time salary the pay actually is.
c Some people waste time applying for jobs because they don't read the advert carefully enough.
d This phrase is a waste of space because this characteristic is always useful.
e If you see this phrase, make sure you ask what the actual salary is as soon as possible.
f It's important to notice this phrase because it means the job is temporary.
g This phrase could mean the job has unsociable hours.
h If you see this, you cannot be sure exactly how much you will earn.

From *English at Work* © Cambridge University Press 2011 **PHOTOCOPIABLE** (17)

2b Job adverts

Type of activity
Reading and discussing job adverts; listening and noticing job-related vocabulary. Individual and group work.

AECC reference
Rt/E3.7a; Sd/E3.1d; Rt/L1.5a; Sd/L1.2a

Aims
To develop learners' ability to understand job adverts.

Vocabulary
logistics, temporary, permanent, logistics, desirable, essential, qualifications

Preparation
Photocopy one worksheet for each learner.

Differentiation
Stronger learners: ask them to try and guess the meaning of the vocabulary in task 3 from context before referring them to the definitions.

Weaker learners: talk them through the job ads, discussing what each job is advertising, before doing task 1.

Warmer
Ask the learners where they can find job adverts, and what the ads normally ask you to do if you want to apply.

1 Give each learner a worksheet. Ask learners to look at the ads quickly to see if they'd be interested in applying for any of them. Conduct feedback.

2 Ask learners to work in pairs to answer these questions.

> **Answers**
> **a** 1
> **b** 2 and 4
> **c** 2
> **d** 1 and 2
> **e** 1 = apply online; 2 = phone for an application pack; 3 = walk into a Silver Screen Cinema near you; 4 = apply by post

3 Ask learners to work in pairs to find the abbreviations, words and phrases from the texts.

> **Answers**
> **a** K
> **b** ph
> **c** pa (per annum)
> **d** No previous experience necessary
> **e** proven track record
> **f** backshift

4 (▶3) Ask learners to read the question and then play the recording.

> **Answers**
> **1** warehouse manager

5 (▶3) Ask learners if they can remember or work out the missing phrases from the conversation, and write them in the gaps. Point out that the first letter of each word is provided. Play the recording again if necessary for the learners to check.

> **Answers**
> **a** work-life balance.
> **b** career change
> **c** like the sound of
> **d** cut out
> **e** relevant experience
> **f** transferable skills

6 Ask learners to work in pairs to discuss the advantages and disadvantages of each job from task 1. Conduct feedback by asking learners to share their ideas with the whole class.

Extension
Give the learners a page of up-to-date job ads from a local paper in the learners' own town for them to discuss and apply for if they wish.

Links to other themes in this book
For more on describing jobs, see 4b. For more on looking for and applying for work, see 1 and 3.

> **Answers: Self-study exercises**
> **1** 1 pa; CRB
> 2 IT; K

1 Look at the four job adverts. Would you be interested in applying for any of them?

1

DGP Recruitment

Location	Wolverhampton, West Midlands
Salary	£21,000 – £28,000 pa
Sector	Transport & Logistics - Warehouse
Job title	Manager
Job ref no	XT96412

Click to apply online now

TEMP to PERM opportunity after 13 weeks.

Candidates must:
* have previous experience working within a chilled operation
* be prepared to work nightshift and backshift

2

Weekend LGV Driver

LGV 2 is essential and ADR Class 3 is desirable.

12 months' recent experience of driving LGV 2, ideally with ADR.

This position is to work weekends; however there are additional hours:
* Saturdays 10 hour day £15.50ph
* Sundays 8 hour day £16.50ph
* Additional hours available Mon–Fri 16:00–22:00 £9.50ph
* An advanced Criminal Records Bureau check will be required.

There will be three days of training and induction.

For more information and an application pack, please contact John Hawe by phone on 01151 882 356.

3

Hi there. Have you got what it takes? Are you a people person? And are you passionate about film? Then maybe you'd like to join our fun-loving team at your local Silver Screen Cinema! We have loads of vacancies, from ushers to vendors. Pay dependent on age and experience. So why not just pop into your local Silver Screen Cinema for a chat with the manager?

4

personal trainer / fitness instructor

Are you enthusiastic about sport, health and fitness? Then a career in Personal Training could be for you. We invite applications from highly motivated individuals with a proven track record of success. Starting salary OTE £21K to £29K. No previous experience necessary: through our Fast Track Scheme you can gain recognised qualifications in Sports Nutrition, Exercise to Music and more. Applications by post to HR Director, Oxley Personal Fitness Solutions, 247 Trout Lane, Monkton, MK2 8QL.

2 Read the adverts again and answer these questions.

a Which job is for a limited period at first?
b Which jobs include training?
c Which job do you need to have qualifications for?
d Which jobs do you need to have experience for?
e What do you need to do to apply for each job?

3 Find abbreviations, words and phrases from the adverts which mean the following.

a thousand pounds
b per hour
c per year
d You do not need to have done this job before.
e You need to be able to show that you have done well in the past.
f a workshift from late afternoon until late evening

4 Listen to two friends discussing the adverts. What job is the man interested in?

5 Listen again and complete the lines from the conversation.

a Got to think about the w.................. b..................., don't want to be working all the time. No, that's it. No more driving for me.
b Time for a c.................. c..................., then, is it?
c So which one do you l.................. t.................. s.................. o..... ? What about the job as a trainer?
d I'm just not c.................. o.................. for that kind of work. Stuck in the gym all day, no...
e Well, no offence, but you haven't got any r.................. e.................., have you?
f But I've got all the t.................. s.................. from my work with logistics.

2c Applying in writing for a job

Type of activity
Applying guidelines for writing job applications.
Individual and pair work.

AECC reference
Wt/E3.1a; Wt/L1.3a

Aims
To develop learners' ability to compose coherent text and write a successful job application letter.

Vocabulary
specific, refer to, concise, formal

Preparation
Photocopy one worksheet for each learner. If possible, photocopy and enlarge the grid with Louise's letter onto an OHT for discussion and feedback for task 3.

Differentiation
Stronger learners: ask them to write a letter of application for the job in task 3, before doing task 3 itself.

Weaker learners: give them the answer to task 3 and work through it with them, eliciting why one option is better than the other.

Warmer
Ask the learners when they last applied in writing for a job, and what was difficult about it. Tell them that the aim of the lesson is to enable them to plan and write an effective letter of application.

1 Give each learner a worksheet. Ask learners to join the sentence halves and make the guidelines, and then check answers in pairs.

> **Answers**
> **1** d **2** g **3** c **4** f **5** b **6** a **7** e

2 Ask learners to critically discuss the advice with a partner, and talk about how useful each piece of advice would be to them. Conduct feedback.

3 Elicit that Louise needs to write a letter of application to apply for the job. Explain that there are alternative phrases for each part of Louise's letter, and that they should choose which phrase is best. Do 1 together as an example, and then ask learners to work in pairs to complete the rest of this task.

> **Answers**
> **1** a **2** a **3** b **4** b **5** a **6** b **7** a **8** b
> **9** b **10** b **11** a

4 Ask learners to refer back to the guidelines and consider which Louise has followed.

> **Answers**
> all of the guidelines

5 Ask learners to work alone and write a letter of application, using Louise's letter as a model (see Extension below).

Extension
In order for the writing task to be as realistic and motivating as possible, try to encourage learners to select a job advert that they would genuinely be interested in. You could refer them back to the job adverts in 2b, or ask them to find and reply to a real job ad for a vacancy in their town. Alternatively, you could ask them to write an advert for their ideal job, and then write a letter/email applying for it.

Links to other themes in this book
For more on formal writing, see 6c and 10b. For more on looking for work and applying for jobs, see 1 and 3.

Answers: Self-study exercises

1 Across
  2 childcare
  4 attach
  6 IT skills
  7 communuication

Down
1 job reference
3 concise
5 position

Applying in writing for a job (2c)

1 Join 1–7 and a–g to make seven pieces of advice.

1 If possible, address the letter to a specific person.	a One page with four paragraphs should be enough.
2 Say where you	b not on how it can help you.
3 Make clear exactly which job you are applying for.	c Use the job reference number (if provided) for this.
4 In your letter, refer	d If there's no name on the advert, call the company to find out who deals with recruitment.
5 Focus on how you can contribute to the company,	e how formal (or informal) your application letter should be.
6 Keep your letter concise.	f to the relevant skills and experience on your CV.
7 Use the language in the job advert as a guide to tell you	g saw the job advertised.

2 Which three pieces of advice from task 1 do you think are the most important?

3 Louise Gide is applying for the job advertised below.

TINY TOTS

We specialise in the recruitment of childcare staff for families across the UK. We offer an attractive package, including return flights if coming from abroad and assistance finding English language classes. Previous experience desirable but not essential.

Interested applicants should send a CV and covering letter to Mrs Sally Howarth at TINY TOTS, 24 BAKEWELL LANE, CARLTON, quoting ref. no. TT3958.

Look at Louise Gide's application letter for this job. Choose the best phrase (a or b).

1 (a) Dear Mrs Howarth / (b) Dear Sir or Madam,

2 (a) Reference TT3958 / (b) Job application letter

3 (a) I hope you are well. / (b) I am writing to apply for work as an au pair with your agency.

4 (a) I understand that you have a lot of vacant positions, but I only want to work in London. / (b) I see from your advertisement on the overseas jobs website that you are looking to fill positions throughout the country, and I would be most interested in working in London, if possible.

5 (a) My name is Louise Gide, and, as you will see from the attached CV, I have just finished school in France. / (b) I'm Louise Gide, and I have just finished school.

6 (a) I have never had a job like this before! / (b) Although I have not actually worked with children, I have spent considerable amounts of time looking after my young cousins, nieces and nephews.

7 (a) This has given me childcare skills which would be very useful for a family employing me. / (b) I have always really enjoyed looking after children.

8 (a) As I am a very strong candidate for this post, I hope I will hear from you soon. / (b) If you feel I would be a suitable candidate, I would be delighted to hear from you.

9 (a) I would be very grateful if you could let me know when you would like to interview me for a position. / (b) I would be pleased to have the opportunity to discuss my application by phone or face to face at an interview.

10 (a) Let me know if you'd like to have a chat about anything. / (b) Please do not hesitate to contact me if you require further details.

11 (a) I look forward to hearing from you.   (b) Let's chat soon!
      Yours sincerely,   Cheers,
      Louise Gide   Louise

4 Which of the guidelines in task 1 has Louise followed? Can you find examples?

5 Write a letter of application for this job.

Vacancy for Helpdesk Agent

You will answer queries from customers about online insurance quotes, and advise them accordingly. With a proven track record in customer service, you will also have excellent IT and communication skills. Application by email to manchesterhelpdeskpost@54321job.co.uk, quoting Ref FG23KN93.

3a Interview tips

Type of activity
Exchange of advice for job interviews. Individual, pair and group work.

AECC reference
Lr/E3.5b; Rt/E3.8a; Rt/L1.5a; Lr/L1.3a

Aims
To raise awareness of how to prepare before and how to behave during a job interview.

Vocabulary
anticipate, rule of thumb, date, handshake, first impression

Preparation
Photocopy one worksheet for each learner and cut along dashed lines as indicated, making sheets for Student A and sheets for Student B.

Differentiation
If your group contains learners who have never been for a job interview, you could invite learners who have to describe to them what happened, and how they felt before, during and after the interview.

Warmer
Ask learners what they do to prepare for a job interview.

1 Give each learner a copy of the top part of the worksheet. Refer learners to the pictures and ask them to discuss the question in pairs.

> **Answers**
> The first candidate is preparing for the interview by researching the company, which should increase her chances of getting the job. The second candidate is making a poor impression on the interviewers by turning up poorly presented. The third candidate has also failed to impress the interviewers by talking too much about money.

2 Divide the class into two groups. Give one half of the class Student A's part of the worksheet and the other half Student B's. Put learners in small groups with learners who have the same section. Ask them to read the text, and make notes about the advice given in their text.

3 Now pair up the learners so that they are working with a learner who read the other text. Refer them to the questions on their part of the worksheet, and explain that they should now find out the answers to these questions from their new partner.

4 Discuss the advice given in both texts as a whole class, and ask the learners the following questions:

Which advice do you think is the most useful?

Is there any you do not agree with?

Did any of the advice surprise you?

Which pieces of advice are connected with the pictures at the top of the page?

Extension
Show the learners a clip about job interview advice from a video-sharing website. Then the learners prepare their own presentation or film giving advice for how to succeed at job interviews.

Links to other themes in this book
For more on looking for work and applying for jobs, see 1 and 2.

Answers: Self-study exercises

1 1 finding out / to find out   2 answering
   3 to get   4 to make   5 Asking   6 to relax

2 1 anticipate   2 thumb   3 to   4 positive

1 Look at the pictures of three job candidates before and during their interviews. Do you think the candidates will get the jobs?

Cards for tasks 2–4

✂ . . . .

STUDENT A
Read the text in the box and make notes.

Before the interview

You really need to start preparing several days before the interview itself. The first thing to do is find out as much as you can about the company, so research the company's website fully for this. You also need to anticipate questions they might ask you, like 'Why do you want this job?' Or 'What do you think your strengths and weaknesses are?' Make a list of questions like this, then think about how you would answer them. Practise the interview as well – ask a friend or family member to be the interviewer and ask you the questions. You could even record yourself doing this, and then think about how you could improve. You should also try to think of some questions you could ask the interviewer, as this will show that you are interested.

After the interview

One thing you should do as soon as possible after the interview is write down all the questions you were asked. That way, if you don't get this job, you'll have a better idea of the questions you might be asked next time, so you can be better prepared. And even if you don't get this job, try to remember that everybody gets rejections sometimes. Instead, try to think of every job interview as useful practice for next time!

Ask your partner for some advice.

What should I wear for the interview?   What advice do you have about answering questions?
Do I need to take anything with me?   What advice do you have about asking questions?
How early should I arrive?   Do you have any other advice?

. . . .

STUDENT B
Read the text in the box and make notes.

At the interview

A good rule of thumb is: look smart, but don't wear perfume or aftershave. After all, you're trying to get a job, not a date! And take spare copies of your CV with you, which you can either give to the interviewer or refer to yourself. Leave plenty of time to get to the interview, allowing for traffic delays and getting lost. And remember that the interview itself might be 10 minutes' walk from reception. When you walk into the interview room, remember that first impressions count. Greet the interviewer with a smile and a firm handshake. And if you're asked a difficult question, remember that it's OK to spend a few seconds thinking about your answer before you start speaking. Do try to give positive answers, even if asked about a previous job which you didn't like. Never say things like 'I didn't get on with my boss'. Ask questions if you're invited to, but you probably shouldn't ask about the pay too early in the interview. Some people think it is rude to ask about money until you have been offered the job. At the end, remember to thank the interviewer.

Ask your partner for some advice.

How can I find out about the company?   What if I don't get the job?
How can I prepare for the interview?   Do you have any other advice?
Is there anything I should do after the interview?

3b At the interview

Type of activity
Reading and listening to different answers to the same interview questions; discussing effective (and ineffective) responses. Individual and pair work.

AECC reference
Lr/E3.6a; Sc/E3.4a; Lr/L1.6b; Sc/L1.3b

Aims
To familiarise learners with good interview technique.

Vocabulary
deal with, cut out for something

Preparation
Photocopy one worksheet and one copy of the audioscript (track 4, p. 122) for each learner.

Differentiation
Stronger learners: for the extension activity, ask them to role play an interview for a job of their choice.

Weaker learners: for the extension activity, allow them to do the role play, using the original transcript.

Warmer
As a light-hearted warmer, you could ask learners to imagine and describe how the world's worst job interviewee would perform at an interview. You could then contrast this with the performance of a more successful interviewee. If the learners have recently used worksheet 3a from this book, ask them what guidelines for job interviews they can remember.

1 Give each learner a worksheet. Give them 30 seconds to answer the question. Make sure the learners know what the other two theatre jobs are.

> **Answers**
> Box office assistant

2 Ask learners to look at the conversation. You may wish to read it aloud with another two students. Take the role of Rosana yourself, and try to exaggerate the terse nature of her replies.

> **Answers**
> Rosana is unlikely to get the job based on her performance in the interview, as she has failed to demonstrate that she has the 'excellent communication skills' stipulated in the advert.

3 Ask learners to discuss this question in pairs. Ask learners to share their ideas with the whole class. Discuss Rosana's monosyllabic responses. Elicit more effective answers that Rosana could give, and discuss how these would be better.

4 (▶4) Explain that learners are going to listen to a second version of the interview, in which Mark and Janet ask the same questions, but Rosana gives different answers. Play the recording. Ask the learners whether they think Rosana does better this time, and why.

> **Answers**
> Rosana gives fuller answers; shows genuine enthusiasm for the job; is polite.

5 Give each learner a copy of the audioscript (track 4, p. 122). Ask learners to work in pairs to identify answers they feel are effective, or phrases they feel could be useful for answering interview questions. Ask learners to share their answers with the whole class and discuss why the phrases are effective.

> **Suggested answers**
> I enjoy working with people; I've learned a lot about customer service; that's one of the things that attracts me to the job

Extension
In pairs, learners role play the interview, with the interviewees aiming to emulate the fuller and more positive answers from the second version of Rosana's interview. Invite one pair to perform their interview in front of the whole group, and allow the interviewee's peers to comment on their performance.

Links to other themes in this book
For more on looking for work and applying for jobs, see 1 and 2. For more on improving people's performance in conversations, see 4a and 14b.

Answers: Self-study exercises

1 1 ~~usually you~~ you usually
   2 ✓
   3 ~~decided look~~ decided to look
   4 ~~job most appeals~~ job that most appeals
   5 ✓
   6 ~~you have~~ had have you had
   7 ✓
   8 ✓

2 Students' answers will vary.

1 Rosana has applied for the job advertised here.

Staff with excellent communication skills required to work front-of-house in our busy theatre. Flexible hours. Salary dependent on age and experience. Responsibilities include selling tickets and dealing with walk-in enquiries from the general public. Application by letter and CV in the first instance to the Manager, Everyman Theatre, Hartley, HL7 6TS.

What is the job?

a Box office assistant
b Theatre manager
c Usher

2 Rosana applies for the job and is invited to an interview. Read the conversation. Do you think Rosana will get the job?

Mark: Good morning. You must be Rosana.

Rosana: Yes.

Mark: Come in and have a seat. My name's Mark Pondle, and I'm the theatre manager, and this is Janet Hargreaves, who works with me.

Rosana: Hello.

Janet: Nice to meet you.

Mark: So Rosana, Janet and I are going to ask you a few questions, and then you'll have an opportunity to ask us anything about the role.

Rosana: OK.

Mark: So first of all, why are you interested in this job?

Rosana: Well, I really need a new job, and when I saw this one advertised, I thought, Well, why not?

Mark: Right. And I see from your CV that you're currently working in a hotel as a receptionist.

Rosana: Yes, but to be honest I'm not really cut out for that kind of work. It can be quite repetitive, and whenever a customer complains, or wants a refund, it's always me that has to deal with it.

Mark: Well, this role will involve speaking to the public a lot as well.

Rosana: Yes, but I think that you get a better class of people coming to a theatre.

Janet: Right, Rosana. Have you always been passionate about theatre?

Rosana: Well, I had to read some plays at school.

Mark: Obviously, English isn't your first language, although you speak it very well. But do you feel you'll be able to cope with the demands of the work, dealing with the public and so on, in English?

Rosana: Well, I know my English isn't very good. I make mistakes all the time, and my writing isn't very good. But I think I probably can.

Janet: I see. Now, Rosana, do you have any questions for us?

Rosana: No, but when will you tell me if I've got the job?

3 Work with a partner. Try to suggest better answers for some of the interview questions.

4 Now listen to a second version of the interview where Rosana gives different answers. Do you think Rosana does better this time?

5 Read the audioscript. Underline two things Rosana says which are effective interview answers.

3c After the interview

Type of activity
Listening to a dialogue; making inferences. Individual work.

AECC reference
Lr/E3.7b; Lr/L1.6b; Rw/L1.2a

Aims
To develop learners' listening skills; to encourage learners to see their performance at job interviews from the perspective of an interviewer.

Vocabulary
articulate, express oneself, vague, fit in, comprehensive, typo, achieve, current, know-it-all, attitude

Preparation
Photocopy one worksheet for each learner.

Differentiation
Stronger learners: give them an additional task of preparing answers to the interview questions in task 2.

Weaker learners: give them a copy of the audioscript to help them with tasks 3 and 4.

Warmer
Ask the learners what they think happens after a candidate has just left the interview room after an interview. Explain that they going to listen to two interviewers discussing the three candidates they have just interviewed.

1 (▶5) Give each learner a worksheet. Ask learners to read questions 1–6. Make sure learners understand the questions and the possible answers. Play the recording.

> **Answers**
> 1 a 2 b 3 a 4 a 5 c 6 b

2 (▶5) Ask learners to work in small groups to write the questions the interviewees were asked. Play the recording again.

> **Suggested answers**
> Tell us about your education and working background.
> What do you think your main strengths and weaknesses are?
> Why do you want to work for this company?
> How do you think your current line manager would describe you?

3 & 4 Ask learners to work in pairs to match the words to make phrases (task 3) and then match these to the the definitions (task 4). Emphasise that the definitions refer to the use of the phrase in the context of the conversation.

> **Answers**
> have a quick chat = d
> give a good account of something = c
> do your homework = a
> tick the right boxes = b

5 Ask learners to match the sentence halves and then check their answers in pairs.

> **Answers**
> 1 d 2 b 3 c 4 a

Extension
If you have not discussed the subject already, elicit learner's opinions about who would be most suitable for the job, and what kinds of personalities they think make (or fail to make) good employees.

Links to other themes in this book
For more on looking for work and applying for jobs, see 1 and 2.

> **Answers: Self-study exercises**
>
> 1 1 b 2 c 3 b 4 c 5 a

Don and Jo have just interviewed three candidates for a job in their company, HEG Finance.

Niran Chatree   Angela Bakari   Daniel Smith

1 Listen to Don and Jo talking, and answer the questions.

1 The interviewers are impressed with Niran's
a language skills.
b qualifications.
c CV.

2 Thant's weakness is his
a lack of honesty.
b knowledge of the company.
c understanding of computers.

3 The interviewers think Angela would be
a a good team player.
b nice to the customers.
c highly motivated.

4 The interviewers are worried that Angela
a has had too many jobs.
b isn't a nice person.
c wouldn't fit in.

5 The interviewers think that Daniel
a has a well-written CV.
b has made his CV too short.
c has been successful in his present job.

6 One criticism of Daniel is that he is rather
a ignorant.
b arrogant.
c under-qualified.

2 Listen again. Write down the questions you think Don and Jo asked in the interviews.

3 Match the words from A and B to make phrases from the recording.

A	B
have a	homework
give a	right boxes
do your	good account of (something)
tick the	quick chat

4 Which of the phrases from task 3 mean:

a research a company before the interview
b meet the requirements

c describe something fully and effectively
d discuss something

5 Match the sentence halves to make definitions of the <u>underlined</u> phrases.

1 If someone has _staying power_,

2 When you describe someone as a _know-it-all_,

3 If something is _fresh in your memory_,

4 When _the novelty has worn off_,

a it means that something which used to be interesting because it was new, is no longer interesting.

b you are criticising them for showing off too much about what they know.

c it happened a short time ago, and you can still remember it clearly.

d they have the ability to keep doing something (even if it is difficult), and not give up.

4a Chatting with colleagues

Type of activity
Listening to different versions of conversations to identify polite strategies. Individual and pair work.

AECC reference
Lr/E3.6a; Sd/E3.1a; Lr/L1.6d; Sd/L1.1a

Aims
To give learners practice in making accurate and appropriate contributions to social interactions in the workplace.

Vocabulary
fancy, annoyed, respond

Preparation
Photocopy one worksheet and one copy of the audioscript (tracks 6–7, p.123) for each learner.

Differentiation
Stronger learners: in task 4 ask learners to predict what softening devices could be used before hearing the recording.

Weaker learners: in task 7, allow learners some preparation time to plan what they will say.

Warmer
Ask learners to brainstorm five ways to start a conversation with colleagues, such as 'Alright. How are your children?'

1 Give each learner a worksheet. Ask learners to work alone to choose the correct alternative. Ask them to check their answers with a partner.

> **Answers**
> **a** to meet **b** new here **c** have you worked
> **d** your name is **e** do you do **f** coming
> **g** did you use to work

2 (▶6) Explain that learners will listen to people asking and answering the questions in task 1, but that the answers are not very effective. Ask them to discuss with a partner what is wrong with the response and suggest improvements, using the useful phrases. Play the recording, pausing after each conversation.

> **Answers**
> All the responses are short and do not offer any extra information. In several cases, the speaker tries to end the conversation quickly. They all seem quite rude.

3 (▶7) Explain that you are going to listen to improved versions of the same conversations. Ask students to comment on the speakers' performance, and say how it was better than the first version. Play the recording, pausing after each conversation.

> **Answers**
> 1 The speaker is much friendlier, and seems pleased to meet Ali.
> 2 Although the speaker cannot help, s/he explains the reason, and apologises.
> 3 The speaker gives more information about his job so that it is easier for his colleague to understand.
> 4 The speaker acknowledges that the question was a friendly gesture.
> 5 The speaker avoids making a negative impression by not saying anything bad about the workplace.
> 6 Conchi does not mind that her colleague forgot her name. She makes it easier for him to remember by saying 'Conchi' twice.
> 7 The speaker answers the question, and then asks his / her colleague the same question, allowing the conversation to continue and develop.

4 (▶7) Refer learners to sentence a. Explain that it is correct, but is not exactly what they heard. Explain that speakers often use more words than they really need, adding softening expressions such as 'yeah' and 'right'. Then ask the learners to listen carefully to the recording and add the extra words they hear in sentences a–d. Play the recording.

> **Answers**
> See audioscript (track 7, p. 123).

5 Discuss this question as a whole class.

> **Answers**
> They make the conversation friendlier and more natural.

6 Give out the audioscript (track 7, p. 123). Ask learners to underline phrases (like those in task 4) which do not add meaning, but make the speaker sound more natural.

> **Answers**
> Anyway, oh, to tell you the truth, kind of, really, well, actually, yeah, look, you know

7 Put the learners in pairs, and ask them to role play the scenarios.

Extension
Ask learners to write their own workplace dialogues without any softening devices, and then swap with a partner, who then adds phrases like 'you know', 'kind of' and 'well' to make the dialogue more natural.

> **Answers: Self-study exercises**
> 1 3 6 4 1 5 2
> 2 1 I just put my feet up
> 2 What did you get up to?
> 3 shattered
> 4 catch you later; see you around

1 Choose the correct option. Cross out the incorrect option.

a Hello, I'm Ali. It's nice _to meet / meeting_ you.
b I'm _here new / new here_.
c So what _are you doing / do you do_ in your job?
d Some of us are going for a drink after work.
Do you fancy _coming / to come_?
e How long _have you worked / are you working_ here?
f Sorry, what did you say _is your name / your name is_?
g Where _did you use to work / are you used to working_
before you started here?

2 Listen to seven conversations. How could the responses be improved?

You could try these useful phrases:

Why doesn't s/he say ...?

Doesn't sound very friendly/helpful.

He sounds annoyed.

Why doesn't s/he ask the same question to the other person?

S/he sounds a bit rude.

I think s/he should start her/his answer with 'Sorry'.

3 Listen to a second version of the conversations. Do you think they sound better now? Why?

4 Look at the following extracts from the conversations. They are grammatically correct, but not complete. Listen and write the extra words you hear.

a I'm Robert, but most people call me Bob. Good to meet you, Ali.
b Hello. I'm sorry, but I can't stop, I'm late for a meeting.
c I do maintenance for all the machines, so I need to check if they're all working properly.
d Oh, that's really kind. But I don't drink, so I never go to pubs. But thanks.

5 What is the effect of the phrases you added in task 4?

6 Look at the audioscript. Find and underline other phrases similar to those in task 4.

7 Work in pairs. One of you is Student A, and the other is Student B. Take turns to start these conversations. Remember to speak in a friendly way, and to use natural language.

Student A	Student B
1 It is your first day at work. Introduce yourself to a colleague. ⟶	1 Respond to what your partner says.
2 Respond to what your partner says. ⟵	2 It is Friday afternoon. Ask a colleague about their plans for the weekend.
3 It is Monday morning. Ask a colleague about their weekend. ⟶	3 Respond to what your partner says.
4 Respond to what your partner says. ⟵	4 You see a new member of staff. It is their first day. Welcome them, and tell them about your workplace.
5 Ask a colleague what their job involves. ⟶	5 Respond to what your partner says.
6 Respond to what your partner says. ⟵	6 Tell your colleague about something you did yesterday.
7 You are in the lift with a colleague who you don't know very well. Chat to them. ⟶	7 Respond to what your partner says.
8 Respond to what your partner says. ⟵	8 Ask a colleague to help you with something.

4b Modern job titles

Type of activity
Reading and discussing a blog. Individual and pair work.

AECC reference
Rw/E3.3a; Rt/E3.2a; Rw/L1.1a; Rt/L1.2a

Aims
To raise students' awareness of different job titles.

Vocabulary
horticulture, revenue, hygiene, freelance, rhetorical question

Preparation
Photocopy one worksheet for each learner and provide some monolingual dictionaries for learners to use.

Differentiation
Weaker learners: for task 3, give learners the more traditional titles so that their task is to match the new titles to the old.

Ask learners who work about the job titles they and their colleagues have; ask learners who are not working about the job titles of members of their family.

Warmer
Write on the board *job description* and *job title*. Ask learners what the difference is.

1 Give each learner a worksheet. Ask learners to do this task in pairs.

> **Answers**
> Both business cards are suitable.

2 Ask the learners to read the blog, and decide which business card the writer would recommend for Henry.

> **Answers**
> the first one

3 Ask the learners to work in pairs to identify what the jobs (1–6) actually are. You may wish to provide dictionaries for this task.

> **Answers**
> **1** ticket inspector
> **2** flight attendant
> **3** shelf stacker
> **4** food factory worker
> **5** lollypop man/lady
> **6** cleaner

4 Discuss the writer's attitude and tone as a whole class.

> **Answers**
> The writer thinks these new job titles are a bad idea; he is writing about them in a humorous way.

5 Ask learners to work in pairs to identify which of these feature in the blog. (Make sure they understand that rhetorical questions are questions where no answer is needed.)

> **Answers**
> exclamation marks, strong opinions, humour and rhetorical questions
> (If your learners are familiar with text types, elicit that these are all features of persuasive texts.)

6 Ask learners to read the comments by the visitors to the site and discuss the answers to this task with a partner.

> **Answers**
> Ali, Maria and Bananaman agree; Freddie999, Danny and Boris disagree.

7 Ask learners to write their own contribution to the blog, giving their own opinion. When learners have written their contribution, put them in small groups and ask them to share their contributions and discuss their ideas.

Extension
If possible, bring a list of job titles from the learners' firm(s) or trade(s) for further vocabulary work.

Ask the learners to speak to people they know outside class, find out their official job title, and bring the two most unusual / the two longest to the next lesson.

> **Answers: Self-study exercises**
> **1** 1b 2d 3e 4c 5k 6g 7f 8l 9m 10n 11i
> 12j 13a 14h

Modern job titles (4b)

1 Henry works in people's gardens. Which business card is best for him? Why?

Henry Jones
Gardener

Tel: 07485 398 194
henry@ukmail.com

Henry Jones

Technical horticultural maintenance officer

Tel: 07485 398 194
henry@ukmail.com

2 Quickly read the entry about job titles posted by a blogger called Darren. Which of the business cards in task 1 do you think he would prefer, and why?

If you're using one of these job titles, please stop now!

Let's face it. Lots of people have really silly job titles. Maybe you have. Are you a Customer Development Executive? Or maybe a Revenue Protection Officer? Or maybe, like most of us, you have absolutely no idea what these – or lots of others – actually mean!

But where did all this come from? In the old days, you were a butcher, a baker, a driver or a builder – it was obvious what you did, and that was that. But not any more! You see, a few years ago, some research was done which showed that people would actually rather have a grander job title than a pay rise!

So, instead of being a lorry driver, you can now be a Large Goods Vehicle Driver! Four words instead of just two – I bet you're feeling better already! Fed up with working as a gardener? Don't worry – you can call yourself a Technical Horticultural Maintenance Officer! And you don't even need an office.

We've got a list here of some of some unhelpful job titles. Can you guess what they actually mean?

1. Revenue Protection Officer
2. Air Cabin Crew Member
3. Stock Replenishment Assistant
4. Food Processing Operative
5. School Road Crossing Assistant
6. Hygiene Operative

Posted by Lesley, Leeds
Have your say!

3 What are the more traditional versions of these job titles?

4 What is the writer's attitude toward these job titles? Is the article serious or humorous?

5 People often use blogs to express their opinion about something. Which of the following does Darren use to express his opinion?

| exclamation marks | a balanced argument | strong opinions | humour | rhetorical questions |

6 Look at the comments by the visitors to the site. Who agrees/disagrees with Darren?

Yes. I'm with you all the way. The world's gone mad! *Ali Hussain, Stockport*

Oh, just stop complaining! It's the old job titles that were crazy, not the new ones. I mean, what about 'lollipop lady'? What's that got to do with lollipops? *Freddie999, Merseyside*

I'm not so sure. I describe myself as a Freelance Information Technology Consultant. Perhaps you can think of a better way to describe my work? *Danny, London*

My company recently gave me a new job title, but I just did exactly the same as before. I ended up as Senior Supervising Lead Commissioning Technician. I was in charge of me! *Maria O, Birmingham*

Hi Maria. I think your company just wanted to save a few quid! How did you manage to fit your job title on your business card???!!! *Bananaman, Milton Keynes*

Come on, guys! Times have changed – new job titles just reflect the fact that we live in an information age. What's the problem? *Boris, Bristol*

4c Company structure

Type of activity
Describing company structure. Pair work.

AECC reference
Rt/E3.8a; Rt/E3.9a; Rt/L1.4a; Sc/L1.2b

Aims
To familiarise learners with the terminology for talking about relationships between different departments and levels in an organisation.

Vocabulary
organogram, marketing, finance, HR, payroll

Preparation
Photocopy one worksheet for each learner.

Differentiation
Stronger learners: cut up sentences a–k in task 2 and share out the sentences between a group of learners. They must not look at each other's sentences, and can only complete the organogram by reading the sentences to each other.

Weaker learners: demonstrate some of the target language in task 2 by drawing a simple organogram on the board and describing the relationships in it.

Warmer
Draw a family tree on the board and ask students if they know what it is. Ask them if they know any other uses for this kind of diagram.

1 Give each learner a worksheet. Ask them to say what the chart is and what it shows.

> **Answers**
> an organogram; it shows the organisational structure or hierarchy of a company.

2 Put learners in groups of 3. Ask them learners to use the clues to work out who does which job, and write the names in the correct places on the diagram. Explain that the task is easier if the learners discuss the information and solve the problem collaboratively.

> **Answers**
> General Manager = Ranjit Patel
>
> Marketing Manager = Ivan Glazunov; Shop Manager = Angela Howarth; HR Manager = Mohamed Khan; Head of Finance = Jane Timms
>
> Senior Sales Assistant = David Cuff; Senior Sales Assistant = David Pizorio; Senior Payroll Executive = Malcolm Ax; Payroll Manager = Maria Carter
>
> Sales Assistant= Lisa Hodge; Sales Assistant = Zara Ismail; Sales Assistant = Mike Jones; Sales Assistant (reporting to David Pizario) = Gilbert Brown; Administrative Assistant (Payroll)= Sammi Jatt

3 Ask learners to work alone to write the questions. Monitor and assist learners as required. Then, put learners in pairs to ask each other their questions. Conduct feedback.

> **Suggested answers**
> **1** Who does Zara Ismail report to?
> **2** Which two people have the same level of seniority as the Senior Sales Assistants?
> **3** What is Maria Carter's job title?
> **4** Who is Angela Howarth's line manager?
> **5** Who is responsible for marketing?

Extension
You could ask students about the advantages of a flatter organisation structure, and ask how companies are organised in their countries.

Answers: Self-study exercises

1 ~~compartments~~ departments; ~~report directly at~~ report directly to; ~~responsible of~~ responsible for; ~~at charge of~~ in charge of; ~~line manage~~ line manager

2 1f 2d 3c 4a 5b 6e

Company structure (4c)

1 What kind of diagram is this? What information does it tell you?

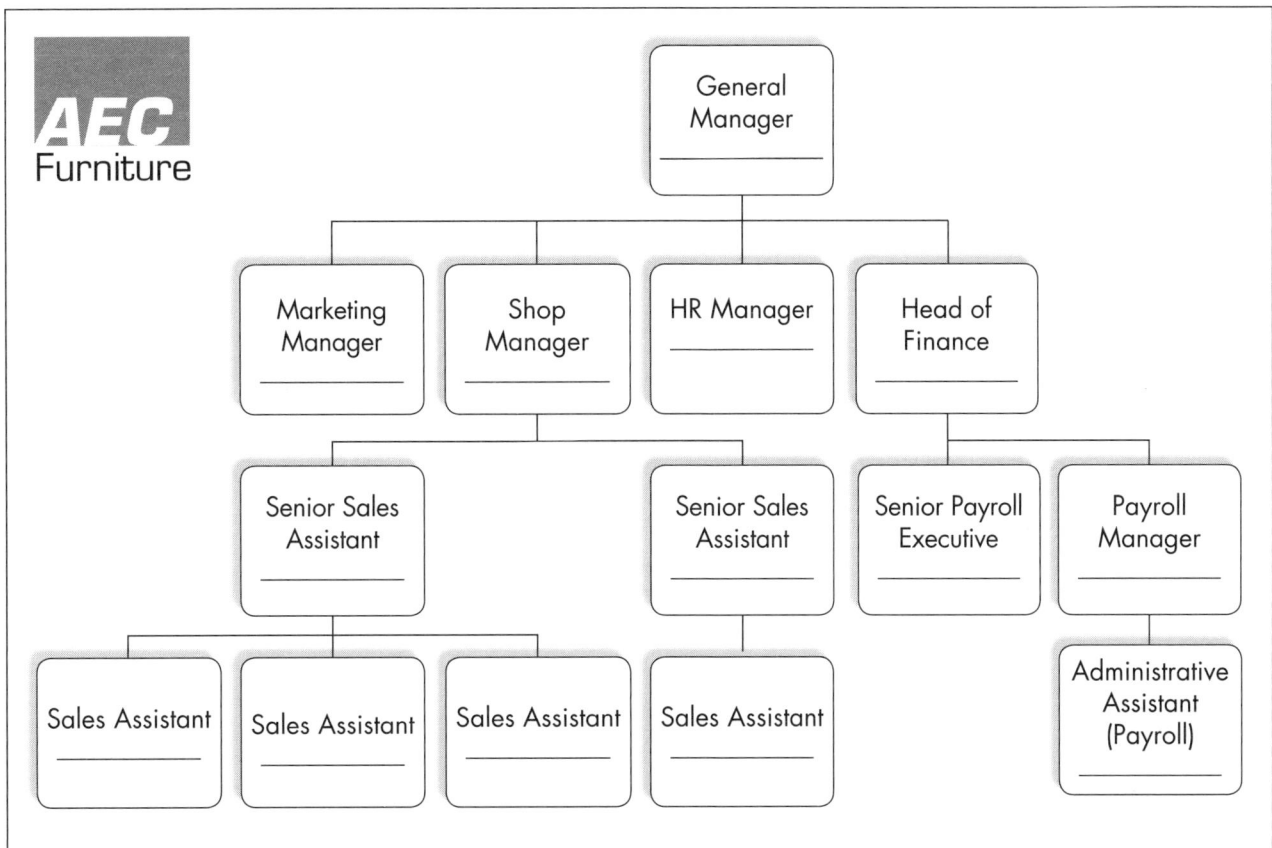

AEC
Furniture

```
                        ┌─────────────┐
                        │   General   │
                        │   Manager   │
                        │ _____   │
                        └─────────────┘
```

Marketing Manager _____	Shop Manager _____	HR Manager _____	Head of Finance _____

| Senior Sales Assistant _____ | | Senior Sales Assistant _____ | Senior Payroll Executive _____ | Payroll Manager _____ |

| Sales Assistant _____ | Sales Assistant _____ | Sales Assistant _____ | Sales Assistant _____ | Administrative Assistant (Payroll) _____ |

2 Complete the gaps above with the names of the staff below. Use the information (a–k) to help you.

Angela Howarth	David Pizorio	David Cuff	Gilbert Brown	Lisa Hodge	Zara Ismail
Mike Jones	Mohamed Khan	Ivan Glazunov	Jane Timms	Malcolm Ax	Sammi Jatt
Maria Carter	Ranjit Patel				

a The Shop Manager's name is Angela Howarth, and she _line manages_ two people called David.

b Gilbert Brown is the only person who _reports to_ David Pizorio.

c Lisa Hodge, Zara Ismail and Mike Jones all have the same _job title_ as Gilbert Brown, although they do not have the same line manager as him.

d Angela Howarth is one of four _senior managers_.

e The other members of the _Senior Management Team_ are Mohamed Khan, Ivan Glazunov and Jane Timms.

f Mohammed Khan does not directly line manage anyone. His job _involves_ dealing with staffing issues, including recruitment and contracts.

g Jane Timms is _in charge of_ the department that deals with payments.

h Malcolm Ax, Sammi Jatt and Maria Carter are _responsible for_ making salary payments to staff.

i Sammi Jatt is _junior to_ Malcolm Ax, but she is not directly line-managed by him.

j Malcolm Ax and Maria Carter are at the same _level of seniority_.

k Ivan Glazunov's _line manager_ is Ranjit Patel.

3 Write down five questions to ask your partner about the staff at AEC Furniture. Use one of the following expressions in each question.

| in charge of | involves | job title | junior to | level of seniority | line manage |
| line manager | report to | responsible for | Senior Management Team | senior manager | |

From English at Work © Cambridge University Press 2011 **PHOTOCOPIABLE**

(33)

5a Agency work

Type of activity
Reading a webpage; writing an email. Individual, pair and group work.

AECC reference
Rt/E3.6a; Rt/E3.7a; Rt/L1.5a

Aims
To develop learners' reading skills.

Vocabulary
permanent, uniform, contract, comply with the law, firm, hire, company, deductions, terms of employment

Preparation
Photocopy one worksheet for each learner.

Differentiation
Stronger learners: if you have internet access during the class, have learners do some further web-based research into the rights of agency workers.

Weaker learners: for task 5, highlight the parts of the webpage where learners can find the answers.

Warmer
Find out from the learners how many of them are working or have worked for an agency. Ask if they can explain what an agency is. Make sure students know that agencies are companies that find staff for other companies. Encourage any discussion about the pros and cons of agency work.

1 Give each learner a worksheet. Ask learners to evaluate Maria's comments in pairs.

> **Answers**
> **a** positive **b** negative **c** positive **d** negative
> **e** negative **f** negative **g** negative **h** negative
>
> (Some learners may see d as positive, but it is below the minimum wage; others may see h as positive, but not having any paperwork could be problematic later.)

2 Ask the learners to read the first paragraph of the webpage, and identify its purpose.

> **Answer**
> to help agency workers (like Maria) know their employment rights

3 Ask learners to make an informed guess here but do not check answers. Make sure the learners are aware of the purpose of this exercise, which is to learn to read efficiently, and find information as quickly as possible by using headings to identify where in a text to look for information.

4 Ask learners to read the full text, and find which of Maria's comments are addressed and where.

> **Answers**
> All of the problems are addressed under the following headings: The National Minimum wage: d; Obligations of your agency: e; Agency worker employment rights: b,d,f; Working hours and rest breaks: g; deductions from pay: h.

5 Ask learners to discuss in groups whether Maria's agency is breaking the law, and if so, in what ways.

> **Answers**
> The agency employing her may be breaking the law in any of the following ways: paying her less than the National Minimum Wage; making her pay for her uniform without making this clear at the outset; withholding payment because the hotel had not paid the agency; not giving her a contract; not giving her a payslip; not giving her at least one free day per week.

Extension
Learners work in small groups to prepare an email to Maria, giving her some advice about what she can do. If feasible, ask learners to write a real email to you on computers.

Links to other themes in this book
For more on getting paid, see 9b and 9c. For more on employment law, see 8a and 11.

> **Answers: Self-study exercises**
>
> 1 The purpose is to persuade job hunters to join Our Job: Your Job.
>
> 2 ~~you finding~~ you *for* finding; ~~deductions your~~ deductions *from* your; ~~a copy your~~ a copy *of* your; ~~comply UK~~ comply *with* UK; ~~entitled breaks~~ entitled *to* breaks

1 Maria has recently started work with an agency. Which of her comments are positive, and which are negative?

a Starting with an agency is a good way to move on to something more permanent later.

b I didn't get paid last week, because the agency told me the hotel where I clean hadn't paid them.

c I just found out the agency expect me to pay for my uniform. That came as a surprise.

d I had to do extra work this week because someone was off sick. That means I haven't had a day off for nearly two weeks.

e I didn't have to pay the agency anything for finding me work.

f I get £5.50 an hour, which is more than I'd get in my country.

g The agency said I don't need a contract. It's just extra paperwork!

h I always just get paid in cash, but never get anything in writing.

2 Read the first paragraph of this webpage about agency workers. What is the purpose of this website?

3 Before you look at the rest of the text, look at the section titles. Which sections will help Maria see if her agency is breaking the law?

4 Now read the webpage in full to check your answers to task 3.

Govinfo
Answering your questions

> **Agency workers – an introduction**

If you're an agency worker (and not an employee), it's important to know your rights and the rules about the way employment agencies and employment businesses should treat you. Do you know what your rights are when you use an agency to find work? Does your agency follow the rules? Many agencies comply with the law, but not all of them. If you are not sure of your rights, or you want more information, you can ring the confidential Pay and Work Rights helpline.

> **What is an agency worker?**

As an agency worker, the firm who hires you pays a fee to the agency, and the agency pays your wages. The agency has to pay you even if the hiring company has not paid the agency.

There are several advantages to being an agency worker. You can:

• use it as a way of entering or re-entering the job market

• use it to work more flexibly to help balance domestic responsibilities

• move jobs easily and with little or no notice.

> **The National Minimum Wage (NMW)**

Most workers are entitled to be paid at least the NMW for all the hours that they work. If your employer deducts anything from your pay, your pay should still be at least the NMW - unless your agency makes limited deductions for accommodation.

> **Obligations of your agency**

Agencies cannot:

• charge you for finding you work

• charge you for your uniform without letting you know they are going to

• make unlawful deductions from your pay

• force you to work more than 48 hours a week

• discriminate against you.

> **Agency worker employment rights**

You also have the right to:

• be paid for all the work you do

• paid holiday

• be paid at least the National Minimum Wage

• protection under health and safety laws

• a copy of the terms of your employment.

> **Working hours and rest breaks**

Your agency, or the company you are working in, can't make you work more than 48 hours a week and you are entitled to at least one day off each week. If you work longer than six hours you should get a 20-minute break.

> **Deductions from pay**

Your agency can only make certain deductions from your pay. You should receive a payslip to show you any deductions that are made, along with how much you are paid.

5b Company policies

Type of activity
Reading a webpage and listening to a phone conversation. Individual and pair work.

AECC reference
Lr/E3.1c; Sc/E3.3c; Lr/L1.6b; Sc/L1.2b

Aims
To develop learners' ability to listen and understand explanations.

Vocabulary
intranet, policy

Preparation
Photocopy one worksheet for each learner.

Differentiation
Stronger learners: after task 4, ask them to use a dictionary to find out what some of the other policies mean, and write definitions.

Weaker learners: for task 4, give them a copy of the audioscript to refer to.

Warmer
Explain what is meant by company policies (rules). Find out from the learners if they know what policies their company has, and where these can be found. If the learners are in a college, and the college has policy documents which the students can access, you could start by showing them these on a data projector. Ask which ones they think are the most important and why.

1 Give each learner a worksheet. Ask them to discuss the question in pairs.

> **Answer**
> a to inform staff about the policies of the company
> b to find out more about the policy
> c students will have different answers
> d recruitment = Vacancies;
>   illness = Sick Leave Policy;
>   money = Payscale;
>   what to wear at work = Dress Code

2 ▶8 Explain that Ibrahim is a new employee and wants to know which policies he should read. Explain that they should tick each of the policies that are mentioned in the recording. Play the recording.

> **Answers**
> Health and Safety; Absenteeism; Sick Leave; Dismissals; Redundancy; Leave; Parental Leave; Appraisal

3 ▶8 Explain to the learners that they are going to listen again to the recording to note down which of the policies Gabby recommends Ibrahim should read.

> **Answers**
> Health and Safety; Sick Leave; Leave; Parental Leave; Appraisal

4 Put the learners into pairs for the role play. For this task, either use the webpage on the worksheet, or, if possible, use the list of policies from the learners' own workplace or college.

Extension
If you have access to a set of college or workplace policies, and feel it would be useful, allocate one policy document to each pair of learners. They have a limited period of time to read through it and prepare a short presentation (maximum 1 minute) on its contents.

Links to other themes in this book
For more on talking about a company, see 4c.

- -

Answers: Self-study exercises

1 1 dismissal 2 employment 3 absent 4 parental
  5 evaluate 6 appraisal

2 1 absence 2 appraise; evaluate 3 parental
  4 employees

Company policies (5b)

IMJC is a catering company based in Newcastle.

1 Look at the page from their staff intranet and answer the questions.

  a What is the purpose of this webpage?

  b Why might someone click on the underlined pieces of text?

  c Does your employer have a similar webpage? Have you ever looked at it?

  d Which policies deal with: recruitment, illness, money, what to wear at work?

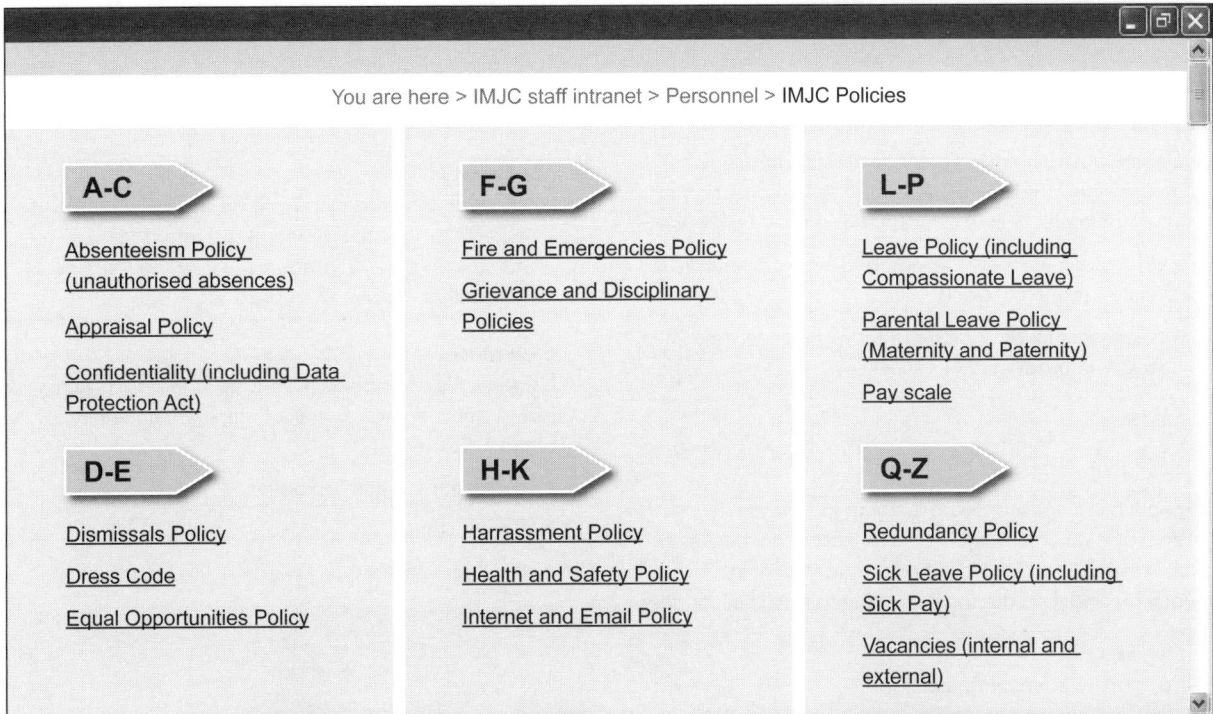

You are here > IMJC staff intranet > Personnel > IMJC Policies

A-C

Absenteeism Policy (unauthorised absences)

Appraisal Policy

Confidentiality (including Data Protection Act)

D-E

Dismissals Policy

Dress Code

Equal Opportunities Policy

F-G

Fire and Emergencies Policy

Grievance and Disciplinary Policies

H-K

Harrassment Policy

Health and Safety Policy

Internet and Email Policy

L-P

Leave Policy (including Compassionate Leave)

Parental Leave Policy (Maternity and Paternity)

Pay scale

Q-Z

Redundancy Policy

Sick Leave Policy (including Sick Pay)

Vacancies (internal and external)

Ibrahim has just started work at IMJC

Gabby works in IMJC's HR department

2 Listen to Ibrahim's telephone conversation with Gabby about the company policy webpage. Put a tick against the policies they mention.

3 Listen again. Which policies is it important for Ibrahim to read?

4 Work in pairs.

STUDENT A	STUDENT B
You are a new employee, and you want to know which of the company's policies and rules you need to know about. Ask your colleague (Student B) from the Personnel Department to explain some of them to you.	You work in the Personnel Department. Explain to a new employee (Student A) which of your company's policies they should read about, and why they are important.

5c Understanding an employment contract

Type of activity
Matching definitions and reading an employment contract. Individual and pair work.

AECC reference
Rw/E3.5a; Rt/L1.2a

Aims
To develop learners' ability to read and understand official language used in contracts and other workplace documents.

Vocabulary
contract, permission, deadline, terminate

Preparation
Photocopy, enlarge and cut up the strips of paper for Task 1 (one set per group of three learners). You will also need to photocopy one worksheet for each learner.

Differentiation
Stronger learners: ask them to try and complete task 4 before doing task 1. They are unlikely to get the answers correct, but they may be able to identify what the meanings of the missing phrases are.

Weaker learners: give them a completed version of the contract, and ask them to use this to help them complete task 1.

Warmer
Find out from the learners:

Do you have an employment contract? Did you read it carefully? What is the most important information in your contract? How much of it did/do you understand?

Explain that the learners are going to learn some phrases commonly used in contracts.

1 Ask learners to work alone to form sentences and then check with a partner.

> **Answers**
> **1** e **2** d **3** g **4** i **5** f **6** b **7** a **8** c **9** h

2 Explain that the learners are going to read an employment contract. Give each learner a worksheet. Ask them to read the questions, read the contract quickly and then discuss the questions with their partner.

> **Answers**
> **a** part-time teaching assistant
> **b** £9.33 per hour
> **c** monthly

3 Ask learners to work in pairs to do this task.

> **Answers**
> **A** Agreement summary **B** Duties **C** Working hours
> **D** Claiming pay **E** Receiving pay
> **F** Probationary period **G** Non-European Union nationals **H** Checks and references

4 Ask learners to complete the contract with the phrases

in italics from task 1. Ask them to check their answers with a partner.

> **Answers**
> **1** with effect from **2** on an as-and-when basis
> **3** under no obligation **4** no later than
> **5** in arrears **6** at source **7** without notice
> **8** authorisation **9** subject to

Extension
Using section headings from task 3 and vocabulary from task 4, learners write offer of employment letters for one of the following:

- a Premier League footballer
- Santa Claus
- the Prime Minister
- their teacher

Answers: Self-study exercises

1 1 as 2 on 3 as 4 under 5 by 6 in
   7 than 8 without

Understanding an employment contract 〔5c〕

1 Join the sentence halves to make full sentences.

1 If you do something on an *as-and-when basis*,
2 The phrase *with effect from*
3 If an event is *subject to* someone's agreement,
4 If you are *under no obligation* to do something,
5 If something happens or changes *without notice*,
6 *Authorisation* means
7 If tax is paid *at source*
8 If you are paid *in arrears*,
9 The phrase *no later than* tells you

a then the employer pays the tax directly to the government.
b official permission to do something, e.g. from the government.
c it means that you do the work first and are paid later, e.g. at the end of the month.
d tells you about the start date of a contract.
e this means that you do it only when the work needs to be done, and not according to a timetable.
f you were not told that it was going to happen.
g it will only happen if that person agrees.
h when the deadline for doing something is, i.e. the last time when you can do it.
i then you do not have to do it.

2 Read Sara Rafsanjani's contract of employment and answer the questions.

a What will her job be?   b What will her pay be?   c How often will she get paid?

Contract of Employment (1) .... **1 September**

(A) _____ Your job title will be PART-TIME TEACHING ASSISTANT. The engagement commences on 1 September and will terminate on 30 July. Your principal place of work will be Oakland School.

(B) _____ In your capacity as PART-TIME TEACHING ASSISTANT, you will be required to provide help as required to the classroom teacher.

(C) _____ The work will be (2).., between the hours of 8 am and 5 pm. The school is (3).. to provide you with additional work.

(D) _____ Your hourly rate will be £9.33. You will need to complete a time sheet each calendar month and submit this to HR (4)... the 4th of the following month. Your payment will be made by the 25th of every month.

(E) _____ Wages will be paid monthly (5) .... by bank transfer. The school has agreed with the Inland Revenue that PAYE and National Insurance will be deducted (6)...

(F) _____ The first 30 days of your employment will be a probationary period. During this period, your employment may be terminated (7) .... by the employer in the case of serious misconduct. Your suitability for further work will be assessed at this time.

(G) _____ If you are not a national of a European Economic Area (EEA) country, you will need (8)... to work in the UK. This is usually through an Entry Clearance VISA in your passport.

(H) _____ Your employment is (9) .... the school receiving clearance from the Criminal Records Bureau.

I hereby confirm that I have read and accept the terms and conditions above.

Signed: *Sara Rafsanjani* (Employee signature)   *Marvin Howardson* (HR Director)

---

3 Write the headings below in the appropriate gaps (A–H) on the contract.

| Duties   Receiving pay   Checks and references   Working hours   Agreement summary |
| Non-European Union nationals   Probationary period   Claiming pay |

4 Complete Sara's contract, using the underlined phrases from task 1.

6a Danger! Understanding health and safety signs

Type of activity
Reading, understanding and discussing common health and safety signs in the workplace. Individual and pair work.

AECC reference
Rt/E3.9a; Rt/L1.3a

Aims
To familiarise students with common health and safety signs.

Vocabulary
cartoonist, extinguish, pedestrian, unauthorised

Preparation
Photocopy one worksheet for each learner.

For task 4, it is useful to have colour copies of the signs. You can print these out from www.hse.gov.uk/workplacetransport/safetysigns

For the extension activity, bring in blank paper and plenty of red, blue, black and yellow pens.

Differentiation
Stronger learners: give them a version of the worksheet with one or more of the meanings (A–H) deleted in task 2.

Weaker learners: give them a version of the worksheet with some of the answers to task 2 already shown, in the form of a line connecting the signs to the meaning. This could be particularly useful if it is done with the signs the learners are unlikely to have seen in their workplace.

Warmer
Show the learners some signs from their own college or workplace. Ask the students what the signs mean, whether they are easy to understand, and why the signs are used.

1 Give each learner a worksheet, and refer them to the title to explain what they are going to learn about. Ask learners to look at the cartoon. Put the learners in pairs, and ask them to discuss questions a–c.

> **Answers**
> **a** 15
> **b** most are not very useful, but students may argue that some are (e.g. 'kitchen', 'drinking water')
> **c** The cartoonist is perhaps suggesting that workplaces have too many signs, and is asking us to think about whether we really need them.

2 Ask the learners to work in pairs to match the signs to the meanings.

> **Answers**
> **a** 2 **b** 6 **c** 3 **d** 4 **e** 8 **f** 5 **g** 7 **h** 1

3 Allow learners a short time to do this task in pairs. In feedback explain that these are known as PROHIBITION, WARNING and MANDATORY signs respectively and using colour signs from www.hse.gov.uk/workplacetransport/safetysigns, explain the coding: prohibition = black picture in red circle; warning = black picture in yellow triangle and mandatory = white picture on blue circle.

> **Answers**
> **a** 2; 6; 7 **b** 3; 5 **c** 1; 4; 8

4 Ask learners to work in pairs and to try and guess what each sign means before the look at the list of meanings.

> **Answers**
> **a** Eye protection must be worn
> **b** Safety gloves must be worn
> **c** Naked flames forbidden
> **d** No access for unauthorised persons
> **e** General danger
> **f** Danger: electricity

5 Ask learners to discuss these questions in small groups. In feedback, ask learners to share their ideas with the whole group.

Extension
Students could design their own health and safety signs, and compare them with the official ones. Encourage them to use the appropriate colours and be creative.

> **Answers: Self-study exercises**
>
> **1** 1 mustn't 2 have to 3 are not allowed 4 must 5 might

Danger! Understanding health and safety signs

1 Discuss the questions.

a How many signs can you see in the cartoon?
b Which of them do you think are really necessary?
c What point is the cartoonist making?

2 Match the signs to the meaning.

a You canot drive industrial vehicles here.
b Do not use water to extinguish a fire.
c Be careful – there is a drop here.
d Pedestrians please go this way.
e Ear protection must be worn.
f Beware – low temperature.
g You cannot walk this way.
h Boots must be worn here.

3 Which of the signs (1–8)

a tell you not to do something?
b warn you about a possible danger?
c say that you have to do something?

4 Look at these other common signs. What do you think these signs mean?

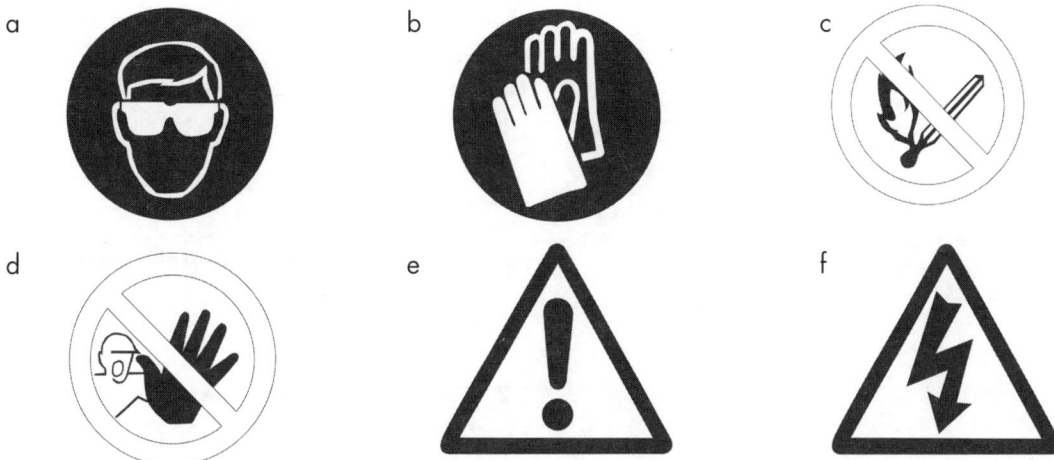

Danger: electricity   Naked flames forbidden   No access for unauthorised persons
General danger   Eye protection must be worn   Safety gloves must be worn

5 Discuss these questions with a partner.

a What health and safety issues are there in your workplace?
b What signs do you see in your workplace? Do you know what they all mean?

6b Health and safety training

Type of activity
Listening to a health and safety briefing. Individual and group work.

AECC reference
Lr/E3.2a; Lr/L1.2a

Aims
To provide practice in listening to a training presentation.

Vocabulary
hazard, burn, scald, trolley, mop, bucket, vacuum cleaner, cable, cleaning agent, slip, mess

Preparation
Photocopy one worksheet for each learner.

Differentiation
Stronger learners: Give them some extra words to listen out for (e.g. trolley, scald, cuppa) and ask them to say what the speaker says about these things.

Weaker learners: allow them to use the audioscript to help them with task 3.

Warmer
Write 'The golden rules of learning English' on the board, and elicit some ideas from the students (e.g. do a little bit of practice every day). Use this to explain what we mean by 'golden rules'.

1 (▶9) Give each learner a worksheet. Explain that the learners are going to listen to part of a health and safety training session. Ask them to listen and complete the golden rules. Play the recording.

> **Answers**
> **a** rush
> **b** things away
> **c** and check

2 (▶10) Ask the learners to describe what is happening in the pictures. Make sure learners know the following vocabulary at this point: *slip, oven gloves, burn, scald, mop and bucket, cleaning agent, spilt, cable, vacuum cleaner*. Set the task and play the recording.

> **Answers**
> **a** 2 **b** 3 **c** 6 **d** 7 **e** 1 **f** 5 **g** 8 **h** 4

3 Divide the class in two. Ask half the class to work in pairs and write a checklist for the restaurant and kitchen staff, and the other half to write a checklist for the housekeepers.

4 Pair up each learner with a learner from the other half of the class. Ask them to share and write down each other's checklists so that both learners have a checklist for both types of staff.

5 (▶10) Explain to the learners that they are going to listen again and check their lists. Play the recording.

> **Answer key**
> RESTAURANT AND KITCHEN STAFF
>
> **Dos**
> • use oven gloves
> • put knives away
> • clear up spilled food
>
> **Don'ts**
> • rush when carrying food
>
> HOUSEKEEPERS
>
> **Dos**
> • put vacuum cleaners away
> • put lids back on cleaning agents
>
> **Don'ts**
> • leave mops and buckets out
> • leave bathroom floors wet

6 Put learners in groups with learners working in similar jobs, and ask them to design a health and safety poster specific to their line of work.

Extension
Learners could be asked to prepare and deliver a short health and safety briefing specific to their work, incorporating some of the vocabulary from this unit.

Links to other themes in this book
For more on workplace training, see 8b.

Answers: Self-study exercises

1 ~~scald~~ slip; ~~slip~~ scald; ~~lying~~ waiting; ~~safety~~ way; ~~waiting~~ lying; ~~way~~ safety

2 1 scald 2 out of harm's way 3 waiting to happen 4 lying around 5 slip 6 safety record

1 1 Listen to the introduction to a health and safety training session at a hotel. Complete the three golden rules.

a Don't ....

b Put ....

c Stop ....

2 Look at the hazards below. What are they? Listen to the recording and number the pictures in the order that they are mentioned.

a

b

c

d

e

f

g

h

3 Work with a partner. Write a dos and don'ts checklist for the restaurant and kitchen staff or the housekeepers (your teacher will tell you which.) Use the pictures above to help you.

RESTAURANT AND KITCHEN STAFF

Dos

....

....

....

Don'ts

....

....

....

HOUSEKEEPERS

Dos

....

....

....

Don'ts

....

....

....

4 Work with a new partner. Complete the other checklist by asking your partner to tell you what they wrote down.

5 Listen again and make any necessary changes to the checklists.

6 Think of some more dos and don'ts for a different job. Design a poster showing your ideas.

6c Reporting accidents

Type of activity
Reading and writing a report. Group and individual work.

AECC reference
Rt/E3.1a; Wt/E3.2a; Rt/L1.1a; Wt/L1.3a

Aims
To develop students' ability to plan and write a report in paragraphs.

Vocabulary
accident, supervisor, witness, electric shock, incident, install, cable, shaken, sustain, injury

Preparation
Photocopy one worksheet for each learner.

Differentiation
Stronger students: give them the email cut up, and ask them to put the text into the most logical order.

Weaker students: for task 5, give the students a specific accident to report that is quite similar to Piotr's; ask them to use Piotr's letter as a model.

Warmer
Ask learners if they know of any examples of accidents that have happened at work. If you have access to the Internet, show them these audio slide shows from Worksafe, British Columbia: www2.worksafebc.com/publications/multimedia/slideshows.asp

1 Put the learners in groups, and ask them to discuss the questions.

> **Answers**
> **a** builder
> **b** e.g. builder, plasterer, electrician
> **c** injuries resulting from use of heavy materials / dangerous equipment
> **d** Accidents need to be reported to a manager.

2 Ask learners to read the email and discuss the answers to the questions in pairs.

> **Answers**
> **a** Piotr is writing to report an accident he had at work.
> **b** He had an electric shock while operating a drill.
> **c** Robert Wilbur, his supervisor

3 Ask the students why Piotr's email is clear and easy to read. Elicit that this is partly because of the logical sequencing of information and clear paragraphing. Refer learners to the descriptions of the paragraphs in the box and ask them to match the descriptions to the paragraph.

> **Answers**
> **1** reason for writing
> **2** brief description of role
> **3** time and place of accident
> **4** description of accident
> **5** probable cause of accident
> **6** what happened after the accident

4 In order to draw learners' attention to some vocabulary from Piotr's email that could be useful in their report in task 5, ask them to work in pairs to complete the sentences.

> **Answers**
> **a** bang **b** occurs **c** suffer **d** sustained
> **e** responsibility **f** by accident

5 Elicit suggestions for other accidents that might occur in the students' workplace(s), e.g. supermarket staff hurt back lifting heavy boxes; bus driver hit a lamppost; cook was scalded by hot food. Ask learners to write a report about an imaginary accident for their manager. Monitor and help with vocabulary as required.

Extension
Students may be interested to see a template accident report form which managers complete in the event of an accident: www.hse.gov.uk/forms/incident/f2508.pdf

Learners could complete a form with the information from another learner's report.

Links to other themes in this book
For more on formal writing, see 10b.

> **Answers: Self-study exercises**
>
> **1** 1 accident happened   2 report the accident
>   3 witnessed the accident   4 by accident
>
> **2** 1 ~~supervizor~~ supervisor; ~~ocurs~~ occurs
>   2 ~~ellectric~~ electric; ~~shacken~~ shaken
>   3 ~~responsibilty~~ responsibility; ~~acident~~ accident
>   4 ~~sustaned~~ sustained; ~~sights~~ sites
>   5 ~~raport~~ report; ~~insident~~ incident

Reporting accidents 6c

Piotr Kowalski works on a building site.

1 Look at the photograph and discuss the questions.

a What is Piotr's job?
b What other jobs do people do on building sites?
c What sort of accidents do people have on building sites?
d What do people need to do if they have an accident at work?

2 Read Piotr's email to his HR Manager, Mr Clore, and answer these questions.

a Why is he writing to Mr Clore?
b What happened yesterday?
c Who witnessed the accident?

To: Piotr Kowalski (Kowalski_P@Construction.co.uk)
From: John Clore (Clore_J@Construction.co.uk)
Subject: ! accident report

Dear Mr Clore,

Following my conversation with my supervisor Robert Wilbur yesterday, I am writing to report an accident which occurred at work. (1)

I work as an electrician on the building site on Harting Street. It is my responsibility to install the lights throughout the building. (2)

At 4:30 yesterday afternoon, I was working on the 3rd floor with my supervisor, Mr Wilbur. I was using a power drill to make a hole in the wall to attach the light fitting. (3)

I suddenly heard a bang and suffered an electric shock. I felt the drill handle get very hot and the skin of my right hand was burnt. I felt very shaken by this incident. (4)

Mr Wilbur said I had drilled into an electric cable inside the wall by accident. The electricity in the building was on at the time, and this is what caused the shock. (5)

On Mr Wilbur's advice, I left the building site and went to see my GP. She examined my hand, and gave me some cream for it, but said that otherwise I was fine, and that I was lucky not to sustain a more serious injury. (6)

Do please let me know if you would like me to provide any more information about the incident.

Piotr Kowalski

3 Look at the paragraph descriptions below. Match them to the paragraphs (1–6).

| description of accident | time and place of accident | what happened after the accident |
| brief description of role | probable cause of accident | reason for writing |

4 Complete the sentences (a–g) with a word or phrase from the box.

| suffer | bang | sustained | by accident | responsibility | shaken | occurs |

a I heard a loud ...., and all the lights went off.
b Staff are required to report any accident that ...., even if nobody is injured.
c We want to make sure that you don't .... an electric shock.
d He fell and .... an injury to his leg.
e It is your .... to ensure that your work environment is completely safe.
f I did something really silly, and locked myself into the storeroom .... I didn't have a key, but I managed to phone security, and they came and let me out.

5 Imagine that you had an accident in your workplace. Write an email about it to your manager.

7a Computer language

Type of activity
Matching definitions to computing lexis. Group work.

AECC reference
Rw/E3.1a; Rw/L1.2a

Aims
To develop learners' vocabulary.

Vocabulary
identify, data

Preparation
Photocopy one worksheet for each learner.

In addition, for tasks 1 and 2, photocopy the same worksheet for each group of three to four learners and cut along the dotted lines to make a set of cards for each group.

Differentiation
IT literacy: reduce the number of terms for those learners not used to using computers.

Warmer
Ask learners to find out from their partner the last three things they did on a computer. Tell the learners that they are going to learn some words connected with computers. Write on the board the following pairs of words:

- internet / intranet
- hardware / software
- install / connect
- drag / click
- download / upload

Put the learners in pairs and ask them to explain the difference between the pairs of words. Conduct whole-class feedback.

1 Explain that learners will have two kinds of cards: small cards (with a word or phrase) and large cards (with a definition). Put learners in groups of three to four and give each group a set of cards. Ask them to match the words/phrases to the definitions.

Answers
see worksheet

2 Give each learner a worksheet. Ask them to work with a partner to test each other. Explain that they should take one worksheet and fold it along the vertical line. They then hold the worksheet between them so that one learner can see the definitions, and the other learner the words and phrases. They should take it in turns to read out a definition or word/phrase for their partner to give the corresponding word/phrase or definition.

3 Ask learners to work alone to complete the questions.

Answers
a files **b** crash **c** login **d** log off **e** intranet

4 Ask learners to work in pairs to discuss the questions. Conduct whole-class feedback.

Extension
Refer technically minded learners to a site such as www.techterms.com, an online glossary of commonly used technical terms, and ask them to find five terms they have encountered but not fully understood.

Answers: Self-study exercises

1 1 intranet 2 login 3 hard drive 4 file
5 reboot 6 hardware 7 database
2 1 b 2 e 3 d 4 a 5 c

Computer language (7a)

Anything that can be saved on a computer, such as a document, photograph or movie.	**file**
The name you use to identify yourself on a computer system.	**username**
A secret word or phrase (often alphanumeric) that you need to access your private email or computer accounts. You can usually change this if you want.	**password**
Details (username + password) which allow you to start using a computer system, email account or website.	**login**
End a session using a computer.	**log off**
A person (usually a manager or IT specialist) who has the authority and know-how to install and uninstall software.	**administrator**
Physical equipment that can be connected to a computer network, e.g. scanner, USB drives, digital cameras.	**hardware**
A private computer network of pages that can only be accessed from computers within the network. Many colleges and large companies have these.	**intranet**
The part of your computer that stores data. This data is stored magnetically so that it remains even when the electricity is switched off.	**hard drive**
Remove software that was installed on a computer.	**uninstall**
Switch a computer back off and then back on again – restart.	**reboot**
An electronic filing system that enables you to manage and find information, for example customers' names and addresses.	**database**
A group of connected computers. This allows data on one computer to be accessed from another connected computer.	**network**
Stop working – when a computer does this, it is usually because of some problem. You normally need to restart the computer after this.	**crash**
A central computer from which other computers get information.	**server**

3 Put the letters in the right order to complete the questions.

a Do you always remember to back up your .... (S E F L I) ?

b How often does your computer .... (S H A R C) ?

c Do you ever forget your .... (G L O I N) details? What can you do to find them?

d How often do you forget to .... (F G L O O F) after using the computer?

e Does your company have an .... (N T T I N R A E)? What is it used for?

4 Work with a partner. Ask and answer the questions in task 3.

7b Computer maintenance

Type of activity
Reading a webpage. Individual work.

AECC reference
Rt/E3.3a; Rt/L1.4a; Ws/E3.1a; Ws/L1.2a

Aims
To develop learners' gist and detail reading skills.

Vocabulary
fix, troubleshoot, invest, store, audible, modem, server, crash, keep (happening)

Preparation
Photocopy one worksheet for each learner.

Differentiation
IT literacy: pair up regular computer users with those who are not computer literate. For task 5, offer learners who are not very computer literate the option of giving advice about something different (e.g. cooking, cars, health).

Warmer
Brainstorm problems that the learners have experienced when using computers. Talk about possible solutions to these.

1 Give each learner a worksheet. Ask them to look at the text and say why it has been written. Conduct feedback, using the answers below, and then ask learners if they feel this sort of advert is effective, and whether it would make them more likely or less likely to contact the company.

> **Answers**
> The page has been produced by a computer repair company. The writer has a dual purpose: to provide tips to help people deal with their own computer problems, and to advertise the company's services.

2 Ask the learners to do this task alone and then check answers with a partner.

> **Answers**
> **1** d **2** a **3** b **4** e **5** c

3 Ask learners to work in pairs to decide whether the sentences (a–e) represent what is said in the paragraphs.

> **Answers**
> **a** Y **b** Y **c** Y **d** N **e** N

4 Point out that the website has various examples of different ways to make suggestions. Ask learners to work in pairs to link the phrases to create seven ways of making suggestions.

> **Answers**
> One option is to check
> Another thing to do is to check
> All you need to do is (to) check
> This can be fixed by checking
> You might want to check
> What you should do is check
> It's always an idea to check

5 Ask the learners to write a similar article with helpful advice about how to keep another piece of workplace equipment running. Put learners in small groups to plan what they will write. You many wish to set the actual writing of the article for homework.

Extension
Ask learners to prepare an email explaining a problem they have with their computer and asking for advice.

> **Answers: Self-study exercises**
> **1** ~~acces~~ access; ~~disconected~~ disconnected; ~~uninstal~~ uninstall; ~~necesarily~~ necessarily; ~~comon~~ common
> **2** 1 ~~What do you want~~ What you want
> 2 ~~need doing~~ need to do
> 3 ✓
> 4 ✓
> 5 ~~always the idea~~ always an idea
> 6 ✓

1 Look at the webpage. What do you think the writer's purpose was?

whatswrongwithmycomputer.co.uk

Home | **Service Area** | **Helpful Hints** | **About** | **Store** | **Contact**

Don't worry – we've heard it all before! We'll be happy to come to fix any problems. But to save you time and money, here are some troubleshooting tips for you.

Top five computer problems

1 _____

This is very common, and it can be caused by a number of factors. To stop it from happening, one option is to invest in more RAM (memory) – this should speed up a sleepy machine. Another thing to do is check what you're storing – do you really still need all those old folders? Alternatively, is there any redundant software that you could uninstall?

2 _____

If you can hear something, there's probably a problem with one of the moving parts in your computer or some other piece of hardware, such as the disks in the hard drive, or one of the fans. You might want to shut down the machine and reboot it. If it's still audible, get it checked.

3 _____

What you should do is start by checking whether your modem's plugged in and switched on.

And of course it's always an idea to ask someone at the next desk whether or not they can access the Internet. If they can't, it may just be that there are problems with your server.

4 _____

This is generally not as bad as people think. Your computer can tell the right time, even when it's been disconnected for hours or even days, because of something called the CMOS battery inside. All you need to do is replace this.

5 _____

People often think that if a computer is crashing on a regular basis, then it means it's time to upgrade to a newer, better one. But not necessarily: as computers get used, they basically get tired and dirty. In most cases, this can be fixed by having a tune-up. Think of it as the equivalent of an annual service for your bike, or an MOT for your car.

Anyway, for these or any other problems, Whatswrongwithmycomputer can be relied on for fast, friendly and reasonably priced service.

2 Match the headings to the paragraphs.

a **What's that horrible noise?**
b **I can't get online.**
c **Why does everything keep freezing?**
d **My computer is running slowly.**
e **The clock keeps going wrong.**

3 Do the paragraphs say these things? Answer yes (Y) or no (N).

a Paragraph 1: There are three different solutions.
b Paragraph 2: Restarting the computer might help.
c Paragraph 3: See if a colleague has the same problem.
d Paragraph 4: This is a serious problem.
e Paragraph 5: If this happens, it's time to buy a new computer.

4 Complete the seven ways to make suggestions (used by the website writer) by linking a phrase in A with one in B, and choosing the appropriate verb form in C.

A	B	C
One	want	to check
Another thing	an idea	check
All you need to	option is	checking
This can	be fixed by	
You might	should do is	
What you	do is	
It's always	to do is	

7c IT helpdesk

Type of activity
Listening to a phone call; role playing of phone conversation. Individual and pair work.

AECC reference
Lr/E3.2b; Sc/E3.3c; Lr/L1.2a; Sc/L1.3d

Aims
To develop learners' ability to ask for and give help on the phone.

Vocabulary
attachment, download, forward, laptop, screen, plug in, freeze

Preparation
Photocopy one worksheet for each learner. Cut off the final section, and cut this up in preparation for task 4.

Differentiation
Stronger learners: for task 2, ask them to note not only which suggestions Jackie makes, but also the language she uses to make them.

Weaker learners: ask them to just do one of the role plays in task 4, and allow them extra time to prepare and make notes.

Warmer
Ask learners if they ever have to contact the IT helpdesk at work. Explain the role of helpdesk to learners who are unfamiliar with it.

1 Give each learner a worksheet and discuss the picture as a whole class, eliciting suggestions from the learners.

> **Possible answers**
> a frustrated, fed up, annoyed. Perhaps his computer has crashed / been damaged by a virus.
> b Maybe he has lost some data, or doesn't know how to do something on the computer and needs help. Or he could have received some bad news in an email.

2 (▶11) Ask learners to read through the suggestions and explain that they should listen for the ones Jackie mentions. Play the recording.

> **Answers**
> a ✓ b ✗ c ✓ d ✗ e ✗ f ✓

3 (▶11) Ask learners to proof-read the text and identify the correct places for the vocabulary in bold. Play the recording again if necessary.

> **Answers**
> a ink levels
> b pop-up message
> c attached document
> d cut and paste
> e administrator privileges

4 Put learners in pairs, and ask them to rehearse the different dialogues. Make sure they swap roles. You could distribute copies of the audioscript for learners to refer to, and encourage them to use language from this lesson in their dialogue. Invite a pair of strong students to perform their dialogue in front of the class.

Extension
Ask the learners to send a follow-up email to the colleague they spoke to in task 4, summarising the problem, the advice, and what happened next.

Links to other themes in this book
For more on dealing with problems, see 6c, 9c and 10.

> **Answers: Self-study exercises**
>
> 1 1 pop-up message 2 admin rights 3 attached document 4 cut and paste 5 ink levels
> 2 1 b 2 d 3 c 4 a

1 Look at the picture and answer the questions.

  a How is the man feeling?

  b What might have happened?

2 Listen to Stefan phoning the IT helpdesk to report a problem with his email account. Which of the following does Jackie, from the IT helpdesk, suggest that Stefan should do?

  a check the printer

  b connect to a different printer

  c attempt to open a file sent with another email

  d search on the Internet for a solution to the problem

  e restart his computer

  f send her the email

3 Read the sentences from the conversation. The underlined phrases are in the wrong place. Cross them out and put them in the right sentences.

  a Well, have you checked if the printer's OK? The _admin rights_ might be too low, that sort of thing…

  b I get a _cut and paste_ saying there's some error.

  c No, that's OK, it's letting me download the _ink levels_ no problem.

  d Well, what about, why don't I go back to the error message, _attached document_, and google it?

  e Our system only allows someone with _pop-up message_ to download anything.

4 Your teacher will give you a role card. Role play the situation with your partner.

Student A: You have a computer problem and need help from Student B.

Student B: You work on the IT helpdesk. Find out about Student A's problem, and offer them advice.

Role cards for task 4

Situation 1 STUDENT A	**Situation 1** STUDENT B
Tell IT helpdesk what's wrong. **Problem:** Laptop screen too dark to see	You work for IT helpdesk. Listen to the problem and offer some advice. **Check:** Laptop plugged in? **Try:** Change settings (from START menu)
Situation 2 STUDENT A	**Situation 2** STUDENT B
Tell IT helpdesk what's wrong. **Problem:** Not receiving emails	You work for IT helpdesk. Listen to the problem and offer some advice. **Check:** Inbox full? **Try:** Delete old messages
Situation 3 STUDENT A	**Situation 3** STUDENT B
Tell IT helpdesk what's wrong. **Problem:** Received a pop-up message saying 'This operation cannot be completed'; computer frozen	You work for IT helpdesk. Listen to the problem and offer some advice. **Check:** Click 'OK' **Try:** Save data and restart computer

8a Case studies

Type of activity
Discussion. Individual and group work.

AECC reference
Rt/E3.4a; Rt/L1.5a; Sd/E3.1d; Sd/L1.2a

Aims
To develop learners' skills in listening to each other.

Vocabulary
court, illegal, army, homosexual, transexual, chaperone, patient, pregnant

Preparation
Photocopy one worksheet for each learner. Cut off the bottom half of the worksheet to give to the learners at the end of the class. Make separate copies of the five case studies (one for each group of four learners) and cut these up.

Differentiation
Stronger learners: give them the longer case studies to read to their group in task 4.

Weaker learners; provide them with clarification strategies (*can you say that again, please; can you speak more slowly, please?*) to help them during task 4.

PLEASE NOTE: the case studies contains references to homosexuality and transsexualism.

Warmer
Ask learners what they understand by equal opportunities. Elicit that this is the principle that everyone should be treated fairly regardless of their race, religion, gender, sexual orientation, or any disability they may have. Elicit that when this does not happen we call it discrimination.

1 Ask learners to match the words to the definitions and check their answers with a partner.

> **Answers**
> **1** c **2** d **3** a **4** b

2 Explain that learners will discuss some disputes between employers and employees. Ask them to say when they would use each of the phrases.

> **Answers**
> To introduce a case: a; d
> To respond to a case you hear about: b; c; e

3 Put learners in groups of four and give each student in each group a different case-study card. Ask them to read the case and prepare to explain it to the others in their group, using some of the phrases on the worksheet.

4 Ask learners to take turns to summarise their case study for their group. Each group should then discuss what they think the outcome of the tribunal was.

5 Ask the class to report back on their discussions for each case. Tell learners what happened in each case (see answers below) Invite learners to comment on whether they feel the outcomes were fair.

> **Answers**
> Case 1: V was successful in his action against the army, and was awarded £35,000 in compensation.
>
> Case 2: W's former employer was found guilty of sex discrimination. W received £25,000 compensation.

> Case 3: X's claim was unsuccessful. Although transsexuals' rights are protected under the Sex Discrimination Act, the employer was still entitled to reject X's application. The Tribunal accepted the nursing home's argument that X was not qualified or experienced enough for the job.
>
> Case 4: Y won his case, but was awarded only the minimum-level compensation of £750, which he did not accept, saying he did not want to accept money which could be spent on the NHS.
>
> Case 5: Z's claim was successful.

Extension
Ask learners to research any other similar cases where employees took their employers to an employment tribunal, and report back to the class.

Links to other themes in this book
For more on employment law, see 5a and 11.

> **Answers: Self-study exercises**
>
> **1** 1 legality 2 homosexuality 3 recruitment
> 4 transsexual 5 discrimination 6 pregnant
>
> **2** 1 recruitment 2 discrimination 3 transsexual
> 4 homosexual

1 Match the <u>underlined</u> words to their definitions.

1 An employment *tribunal*
2 When someone is *dismissed* or *sacked*,
3 An *act*
4 To *legalise* something

a is a law made by Parliament.
b means to change the law, so that something that was illegal, now becomes legal.
c is a type of court that deals with legal arguments between employees and employers.
d it means they lose their job because they did something wrong.

2 Your teacher will give you some examples of disputes between employers and employees which went to an employment tribunal. Which of these phrases could you use to introduce a case, and which could you use to respond to a case you hear about?

a I was just reading about this man/woman who …
b Really, that's unbelievable.
c That seems fair enough to me.
d Did you hear about the case of a guy/woman who …?
e That seems reasonable.

3 Read your card and prepare to explain the case to your group.

4 Work in groups and discuss each case of discrimination.

5 Now listen to your teacher, who will tell you what happened in each case.

Case study cards for task 3

Case 1
V was in the army for eight years, and then left. He claims he was dismissed because he is homosexual, and that his employer (the Ministry of Defence) broke the law by sacking him.

Note: Homosexuality used to be illegal in the armed forces (army, navy and air force), but in 2000 it was legalised.

Case 2
W used to work as an accountant for a manufacturing company. After she left the firm, a man took over her job. She later found out that he was being paid £8,000 per year more than she had received, as well as extra benefits. She accused her former employer of sexual discrimination, and took them to the Employment Tribunal.

Note: Under the *Equal Pay Act*, employers must pay men and women the same for doing the same work.

Case 3
X is a transsexual. Although she had no qualifications or experience in nursing, X applied for a job in a nursing home but was rejected. She believed she was rejected because of her transsexualism, and took the nursing home to the tribunal.

Note: Transsexuals are people who identify with the opposite gender, e.g. a woman who would like to be a man. There is a UK law called the *Sex Discrimination Act*. This makes it illegal for employers to treat someone differently because they are transsexual or because they have had or want to have a sex change.

Case 4
Y, a male nurse, left the nursing profession after accusing the National Health Service of treating male and female nurses differently. In some situations, a male nurse needs a female chaperone when treating female patients. Y argued that this was sexual discrimination.
Note: There is a UK law called the *Sex Discrimination Act*. This makes it illegal for employers to treat men and women differently regarding recruitment, promotion and training.

Case 5
Z, a 33-year-old hotel employee, told her line manager that she was pregnant. A week later, she was invited to a meeting, where she was told she was dismissed. She is taking her employer to the tribunal. The employer claims that they had already decided that the woman's position was to be terminated before they were told about the pregnancy.

Note: It is illegal for a woman to be sacked because of her pregnancy. This would be sex discrimination.

8b Disability Discrimination Act

Type of activity
Listening to a conversation and answering multiple-choice questions. Individual and group work.

AECC reference
Lr/E3.7b; Lr/E3.6a; Lr/L1.1a

Aims
To develop students' listening skills and raise awareness of the Disability Discrimination Act (DDA).

Vocabulary
discriminate, illegal, ramp, obliged, assume, stuff, loads of

Preparation
Photocopy one worksheet for each learner.

If you want to read up on the DDA before the class, the following site is recommended:

www.direct.gov.uk/en/DisabledPeople/RightsAndObligations/DisabilityRights/DG_4001068

Differentiation
Stronger learners: during task 4, ask them to listen out for specific examples of how Aziz can help customers with disabilities.

Weaker learners: give them a copy of the audioscript to check their answers for task 4.

Warmer
Elicit from the learners any disabilities they can name or describe in English. Ask if they are aware of the Disability Discrimination Act.

1 Give each learner a worksheet. Ask learners to do task 1 alone, checking their answers with a partner. When checking answers as a class, refer students to the photos showing a wheelchair, a hearing aid and a guide dog.

> **Answers**
> **a** limited mobility
> **b** impaired hearing
> **c** visually impaired
> **d** disabilities

2 Ask learners to discuss these questions in pairs. Emphasise that if the learners do not know the answer, they should discuss whether they think the answers *should* be true or false.

> **Answers**
> **a** True
> **b** False
> **c** True
> **d** False

3 Ask learners to read the email and answer the questions.

> **Answers**
> **a** to inform staff about DDA training which they must attend
> **b** learners' suggestions will differ (e.g. it will help staff give a better service to customers with disabilities)

4 (▶12) Ask learners to read through the questions and answers and make sure they understand them. Play the recording. Ask learners to check their answers in pairs.

> **Answers**
> **1** c **2** c **3** a

5 Discuss these questions as a whole class.

Extension
You could ask the learners to find out about provision made for disabled people in a place other than their place of work, for example a local college, shopping centre or railway station.

Links to other themes in this book
For more on speaking with managers, see 9b and 10a. For more on workplace training, see 6b.

Answers: Self-study exercises

1 1 impaired 2 limited 3 hearing 4 advised
  5 running

2 ~~oportunities~~ opportunities; ~~appliccation~~ application; ~~disabilty~~ disability ~~impared~~ impaired; ~~Discrimnation~~ Discrimination; ~~disabeld~~ disabled

---

Disability Discrimination Act

1 Write the words and phrases below in the correct gap.

visually impaired   disabilities   limited mobility   impaired hearing

a People with .... may use a wheelchair.
b People with .... may use a hearing aid.
c People who are .... may have a guide dog.
d The Disability Discrimination Act (DDA) is a law which supports all people with ....

2 How much do you know about the DDA? Choose the correct answer.

a Under the DDA, discriminating against somebody because of their disability (e.g. by not giving them a job interview) is illegal. TRUE / FALSE.
b Under the DDA, a firm must have a fixed percentage of employees who have a disability. TRUE / FALSE.
c Under the DDA, all businesses and organisations must make 'reasonable adjustments' to allow disabled people to use their services. An example is fitting a ramp for wheelchair users to get into a building easily. TRUE / FALSE.
d All employers in the UK are obliged to give staff regular training on the DDA. TRUE / FALSE.

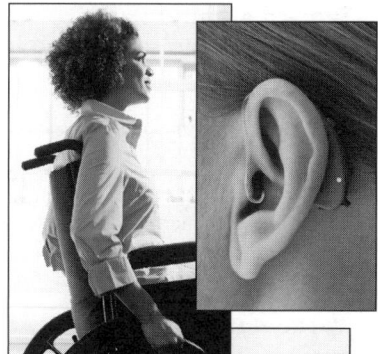

3 Jermaine Thomas, General Manager of Nice Price Supermarkets, sends this email to his staff. Answer the questions about the email.

```
◉ ◉ ◉                                                    ◯
  From:  Jermaine Thomas, General Manager [j.thomas@niceprice.co.uk]
    To:  all staff
Subject:  DDA training

Please be advised that as part of our Equal Opportunities Policy, we
will be running training on the Disability Discrimination Act next week.
This is compulsory for all staff. As you know, a lot of our customers
have disabilities, and we all want to make their experience with us a
positive one. I'm sure you will find it valuable.

Regards,

Jermaine Thomas                      Nice Price
                                        Supermarkets
```

a Why is he writing?
b Why do you think DDA training could be helpful?

4 After the DDA training, Jermaine speaks to Aziz, a member of staff who attended. Listen to their conversation and answer the questions.

1 What is the main thing that Aziz learnt from the training?
 a People in a wheelchair usually expect to be helped.
 b People with a guide dog should get special treatment.
 c Someone's disability isn't always obvious.
2 How will Aziz change the way he works in the supermarket?
 a He will look out for shoppers in wheelchairs in particular.
 b He will start to help people pack their shopping.
 c He will be more aware of shoppers' various needs.
3 Overall, Aziz found the training
 a informative.
 b entertaining.
 c boring.

5 Do you think you would have found the training useful? What could be done at your workplace to give easier access for disabled people?

8c Equal opportunities monitoring

Type of activity
Listening to a discussion and completing a form.
Individual and pair work.

AECC reference
Lr/E3.3a; Lr/E3.6a; Lr/L1.1a

Aims
To provide practice filling in a form; to raise awareness
of concerns and priorities of an equal opportunities
employer.

Vocabulary
*treat confidentially, shortlist, keep something to oneself,
select, ethnic origin, leave something blank*

Preparation
Photocopy one worksheet for each learner. You may
want to photocopy the audioscript (track 13, p. 124–5)
for task 5.

Differentiation
Stronger learners: ask them to attempt task 4 without
looking at the words in the box.

Weaker learners: hand out the audioscript for learners
to check their answers to task 3. Ask them to read it
through before doing task 4 (but do not allow them to
refer to it while doing task 4).

Warmer
Ask the learners to find out from their partner when they
last completed a form, and what it was for.

1 Give each learner a worksheet. Ask learners to discuss
the questions in small groups.

> **Answers**
> **a** Learners' answers will differ.
> **b** for gathering information about the ethnic origin
> of new (or existing) employees, in order to ensure
> that everybody is treated fairly
> **c** Learners' answers will differ.

2 Discuss this question as a whole class.

> **Answers**
> * = compulsory question (you have to fill this in)
> O please click   □ please tick if the answer is 'yes'

3 (▶13) Explain that the learners are going to listen to a
conversation and fill in the form as the speaker on the
recording did. Play the recording.

> **Answers**
> Religion: prefer not to say
> Ethnic origin: (under 'OTHER Please specify') mixed
> Nigerian and Thai origin

4 (▶13) Ask learners to try and remember or work out
the missing words from the conversation, and write
them in the gaps. Explain that you do not expect them
to get all the answers. Play the recording again.

> **Answers**
> **a** suitability
> **b** equal opportunities
> **c** ethnic
> **d** mixed race
> **e** ethnicity
> **f** multicultural

5 Discuss these questions as a whole class. You may
want to hand out copies of the audioscript so that
learners can analyse the language Denise and Gonzo
use.

> **Answers**
> Denise seems in favour (for fairness); Gonzo seems
> against it (he thinks the questions are irrelevant).

6 Put learners in pairs, and ask them to discuss the issues
Denise and Gonzo spoke about, and decide who they
agree more with.

Extension
Many learners will need no help or additional practice at
form filling. However, for those that do, you could provide
them with additional authentic forms as appropriate to
their needs, including those from non-work environments
like a doctor's surgery or a bank.

Links to other themes in this book
For more on form filling, see 9b.

Answers: Self-study exercises

1 complete the form; promote equal opportunities; treat
(something) confidentially; shortlist candidates

2 1 promote equal opportunities
  2 complete the form
  3 shortlist candidates
  4 treat ... confidentially

1 Look at the form and discuss these questions.

a Have you ever had to fill a form like this?
b What do you think it is for?
c How would you feel about filling in a form like this?

SOUTH HIRTON COUNCIL

Equal opportunities monitoring form.

All applicants for a job with South Hirton Council are invited to complete this part of the form. The information will be treated confidentially, and will not be used to shortlist candidates.

Religion
O Christian   O Buddhist
O Jewish   O No religion
O Sikh   O Other
O Muslim   O Prefer not to say
O Hindu

* Ethnic origin
WHITE
O White British   O White Irish
O Other white background
Please specify ....

ASIAN
O Asian or British Asian
O Indian   O Pakistani   O Bangladeshi
O Chinese
O Other Asian.
Please specify ....

BLACK
O Black or black British
O Black African   O Black Caribbean
MIXED
O White and Asian
O White and black African
O White and black Caribbean

OTHER
O Other ethnicity (not listed)
Please specify ....

---

* denotes compulsory field.

South Hirton Council is an Equal Opportunities Employer

---

2 What do the following mean on a form?

*   O (or sometimes ☐ on a printed form)

3 Gonzo recently applied for a job with South Hirton Council, and completed the form. Listen to him talking to his friend Denise, and complete the form as Gonzo did.

4 Complete the extracts from the conversation with words and phrases from the box.

| suitability   ethnicity   ethnic   equal opportunities   multicultural   mixed race |

a Yeah, but the thing is, the stuff they were asking on the form, a lot of it was, like, nothing to do with my .... for the job.
b Well, they always do that kind of thing now, ... monitoring, they call it.
c Anyway, the worst bit was the .... origin section.
d 'Cos I'm ...., you see, my dad's Nigerian, and my mum's from Thailand.
e Well, why should they care about ....? I mean, if you're black, or white, or Bangladeshi, who cares?
f Yeah, well, it's true the council's very .... Got staff from all over the world.

5 Discuss these questions.

a What do Denise and Gonzo think about equal opportunities monitoring?
b What arguments do they use?

6 What do you think about equal opportunities monitoring? Discuss with your partner.

9a Talking big money

Type of activity
Reading and matching definitions. Group work.

AECC reference
Rw/E3.1a; Rw/E3.2a; Rw/L1.2a

Aims
To develop learners' practical knowledge and vocabulary relating to work and pay in the UK.

Vocabulary
tax, summary, period, increase

Preparation
Photocopy one worksheet for each group of three or four learners and cut the word and definition cards up. Also photocopy one worksheet for each learner.

If you wish to read up on National Insurance, PAYE, P45 and P60, the following is recommended:

www.direct.gov.uk/en/MoneyTaxAndBenefits/index.htm

Differentiation
Stronger learners: start by giving them the word cards only and ask them to write their own definitions.

Weaker learners: omit some of the phrases (and their definitions) from task 1 in order to make it more manageable, and/or allow use of a dictionary.

Warmer
Check learners know the following words (*worker, payment, tax, employee, earn, pay, form, employer*) in preparation for the main activity by doing this warmer. Divide the class in two teams and invite one learner from each team to come and sit with their back to the board. Write one of the words on the board for the rest of the class to define without saying the word. The two at the front must guess the word. The first to guess the word gets a point for their team. Once a word has been guessed, the two players at the front are replaced by new players, and a second word written on the board.

1 Explain that you are going to look at vocabulary related to pay at work. Explain that learners will have two kinds of cards: small cards (with a word or phrase) and large cards (with a definition). Give one set of cards to each group of three or four learners and ask them to match the words/phrases to their definitions.

> **Answers**
> see worksheet

2 Give each learner a worksheet and point out that the words/phrases are listed alongside their definitions. Ask learners to fold the worksheet in half along the vertical dashed line. Ask them to work individually and use the worksheet to test themselves on their knowledge of the vocabulary. They can then work in pairs and test each other.

3 Ask learners to work in pairs. Ask them to lay the small cards face down individually on a table. (They will not need the large cards with the definitions.) Explain that they should take it in turns to turn over any two cards, leave them face up, and produce a sentence using them correctly together. They continue until all the words have been used.

Extension
Ask learners to create new cards with words/phrases and definitions based on kinds of payment that are of relevance in their own line of work, e.g. *bill, tip* (restaurant); *quotation, invoice* (repair work / construction); *receipt, refund* (retail).

> **Answers: Self-study exercises**
>
> **1** 1 increment 2 pay scale 3 P45 4 emergency
>   5 deductions 6 payslip 7 financial
> **2** 1 c 2 b 3 a 4 d 5 e 6 f

Word cards for task 1

wages	Money that a worker is paid each week or day (usually used for shop or factory workers).
salary	Money that a worker is paid each month or year (usually used for office or professional workers).
hourly rate	The amount of money paid for an hour's work.
PAYE (Pay As You Earn)	The system that takes taxes directly from your pay to give to the government.
National Insurance	The system in which the government collects money from companies and workers to make payments to people who are sick, old or unemployed.
emergency tax	A special rate of tax you sometimes have to pay, especially when you start a new job. It is higher, but you can usually get the money back if you have paid too much.
advance	An early payment that you may ask your employer to give you before the usual payday.
deductions	All the taxes that are taken out of your pay before you receive it.
pay scale	The range of pay that different people in a company receive.
payslip	A piece of paper that you get from your employer each month or each week, which shows how much you have earned and how much tax you have paid.
P45	A form which you get when you leave a job. It is a summary of how much you earned, and how much tax you paid.
P60	A form which you get every year. It is a summary of how much you have earned and how much tax you have paid that year.
tax year	The period from 6 April to 5 April the next year. Your tax payments depend on what you earn during this time. Also called 'financial year'.
increment	One of a series of increases in your pay.

**2 Fold down the central dotted line. Read the definitions.
Try to remember the words/phrases.**

3 Work with a partner. Make sentences using two of the words/phrases.

9b Getting paid

Type of activity
Listening and correcting details on a pay claim form. Individual work.

AECC reference
Lr/E3.2b; Rw/E3.2a; Wt/E3.5a; Lr/1.1a Wt/L1.6a

Aims
To develop learners' listening, numeracy and form-filling skills.

Vocabulary
procedure, claim, go through, amend, tick

Preparation
Photocopy one worksheet for each learner.

Differentiation
For task 1, group learners who work with those who don't.

Numeracy: allow learners to refer to the audioscript to make the calculations in task 5.

Warmer
Ask learners who work how often they get paid. Ask them what they need to do in order to get paid.

1 (▶14) Give each learner a worksheet. Refer learners to the photo and read the text alongside it. Make sure the learners understand the context. Ask learners to read the questions, and play the recording. When checking answers, make sure learners understand the words and phrases in 1a.

> **Answers**
> **a** in arrears; pay claim form; payroll.
> **b** 1 check his form

2 Ask learners to work alone to identify the correct alternative in the sentences. Ask them to check their answers in pairs. Don't check answers until after task 3.

3 (▶14) Play the recording again for learners to listen and check.

> **Answers**
> **a** what sort of   **b** in what   **c** what that means
> **d** Payroll does   **e** what you're saying

4 Ask students to read the form to find any incorrect details and compare their answers in pairs. Don't check answers until after the listening.

5 (▶15) Tell the learners that they are going to listen to Sophie checking Dariusz's form with him. Ask them to check their answers to task 2 and make any other changes that Sophie suggests. Explain that for the sum claimed box, they will need to make notes and calculate the totals after listening. Play the recording.

a

Name	~~Darek~~ Dariusz	Surname (BLOCK CAPS)	~~Stanek~~ STANEK	NI number	~~5528DS~~ NY 24 03 38 C
Month	December	Job	Kitchen assistant	Employee number (on payslip)	~~NY 24 03 38 C~~ 5528DS

Date DD/MM	Start time	Finish time	Hours worked	Rate of pay	Sum claimed
30/12	5pm	11.30pm	~~6½~~ 6	£6.80	~~£44.20~~ £40.20
31/12	5pm	2.00am	~~9~~ 8½	~~£6.80~~ £10.20	~~£61.20~~ £86.70
				Total	~~£105.40~~ £126.90

Employee declaration
I have worked as claimed above. I understand that making a false claim could lead to disciplinary action. Please tick to confirm the above information is correct. ☑

b To calculate the sum claimed for 31/12, learners first need to change the hours worked to 8½, and then multiply this by £10.20 (8.5 X £10.20 = 86.70)

c sum claimed for 30/12 added to sum claimed for 31/12 (£40.20 + £86.70 = £126.90)

6 Put learners in pairs, and ask them to role play the dialogue between Sophie and Dariusz. Explain to the students that they do not need to remember the numbers exactly (hourly rates, dates, number of hours worked, etc.), but need to practise asking for and giving help politely.

Extension
In pairs, learners could role play a similar conversation between a manager and a new member of staff who is unfamiliar with the employer's pay claim procedures.

Links to other themes in this book
For more on talking with managers, see 8b and 10a. For form filling, see 8c. For numeracy, see 15b, 15c, 16c.

Answers: Self-study exercises

1 payroll; in arrears; payslip; in advance; pay day

2 1 in advance   2 payroll   3 in arrears   4 payslip   5 pay day

Dariusz started his new job as a waiter in the Royal Breakwater Hotel on 30 December. His manager Sophie helps him with the procedure for getting paid.

1 Listen to the first conversation between Dariusz and Sophie on 2 January, and answer the questions.

a Look at the words and phrase below. Which three does Sophie explain to Dariusz?
in advance   in arrears   pay claim form   pay day   payroll   payslip

b What does Sophie offer to do next?
1 check his form   2 fill in his form

2 Look at the sentences from the dialogue. Choose the correct alternative.

a Sorry, *what's the* / *what sort of* form?
b One month *in what* / *what in*, sorry? In arrears?
c Right, sorry, I'm not exactly sure *what that means* / *what does that mean*.
d Payroll? Sorry, could you explain to me what *does Payroll do* / *Payroll does*?
e Right. So, *what you're saying* / *what are you saying* is that I'll be paid for my work in December on about 25 January.

3 Listen to the first section of the recording again to check.

4 Look at Dariusz's pay claim form. Are any of the details incorrect or incomplete?

Name	Darek	Surname (BLOCK CAPS)	Stanek	NI number	5528DS
Month	December	Job	Kitchen assistant	Employee number (on payslip)	NY 24 03 38 C

Date DD/MM	Start time	Finish time	Hours worked	Rate of pay	Sum claimed
30/12	5pm	11.30pm	6½	£6.80	£44.20
31/12	5pm	2.00am	9	£6.80	£61.20
				Total	£126.90

Employee declaration
I have worked as claimed above. I understand that making a false claim could lead to disciplinary action. Please tick to confirm the above information is correct. ☐

.... (employee's signature)

Manager declaration
I authorise payment for the hours claimed. Please tick to confirm this. ☐

.... (manager's signature)

5 Listen to the second conversation between Dariusz and Sophie.
a Complete and correct the form as necessary.
b How did you calculate the sum claimed for 31/12?
c How did you calculate the total claimed?

6 Work in pairs. One of you is Dariusz, and the other is Sophie. Act out the conversation.

9c Payment queries

Type of activity
Reading online postings and their responses. Individual and pair work.

AECC reference
Rt/E3.4a; Wt/E3.2a; Rt/L1.5a; Wt/L1.5a

Aims
To develop learners' ability to read websites for specific information.

Vocabulary
web forum, shift, illegal, helpline, confidential, solicitor, deduct, tax code, hang on to, payslip, record

Preparation
Photocopy one worksheet for each learner.

Differentiation
Stronger learners: draw their attention to the style of writing which is common on such websites and ask them to identify instances where this writing is different from more formal texts.

Weaker learners: draw learners' attention to the key vocabulary for tasks 3 and 4.

Warmer
Ask learners what problems employees sometimes have getting paid.

1 Give each learner a worksheet. Ask learners to work alone to read the postings and identify the correct questions. Ask them to check answers in pairs.

Answers
a 2 **b** 3 **c** 1

2 Ask learners to re-read the website to find the answers to these questions and check their answers in pairs.

Answers
a 1 (It tells him that an employer legally has to give you a break on shifts that are six hours or longer.)
b 3 (It tells her that her payslips contain this information.)
c 1 (It recommends a helpline.)

3 Ask learners to work in pairs to answer these questions.

Answers
a Kelly and Bob
b Lisa
c Bob and Lisa
d Annie and Kelly 89
e Annie

4 Ask learners to write a similar post about a problem related to pay at work. Ask learners to write answers to each other's posts. If possible, learners could do this on computers. You could refer learners to a site such as *www.workworries.com* if they need ideas for possible problems to write about.

Extension
You could encourage learners to visit the websites mentioned in the postings to find out more and report back to the class, or to search for other useful sites.

Links to other themes in this book
For more on getting paid, see 5a. For dealing with problems, see 6c, 7b and 10.

Answers: Self-study exercises
1 1 at 2 on 3 with 4 by 5 at 6 at 7 out 8 on
2 1 b 2 d 3 a 4 c 5 e

Payment queries (9c)

1 Look at the three posts and their answers on this web forum. Match the questions (a–c) to the posts (1–3).

a How long must I wait for my pay?
c How much should I be getting paid?
b Why am I paying so much tax?

Askaboutjobs

HOME | BROWSE CATEGORIES | MY ACTIVITY | ABOUT

Post 1:

I've just started work at a leisure centre. The work's a real laugh but they've told me I'm on £30 a day for a 13-hour shift. And I only get a 10-minute lunch break!!!! Is this even legal? I'm 25.

Cheers, Kevin

Best answer – chosen by Askaboutjobs users

Hi there. In a word, NO! You should be getting at least the National Minimum Wage, even if you are right at the bottom of the pay scale. They have to do this now – it's the law! And if you work more than six hours, they have to give you a break of at least 20 minutes. Also, you might want to check this out for more info: http://www.direct.gov.uk/en/Employment/Employees/TheNationalMinimumWage/DG_10027201

Hope that helps, Annie

Other answers

That's not even £3 an hour! it's illegal to do all those hours with no break! Did they give you a contract? Keep it! Why don't you call the helpline? It's confidential, and they can talk about any aspect of your work that you're worried about. Then you should raise the problem with your manager. And if you have no luck, I'd look for another job! Good luck! Bob

Post 2:

My employer is now three weeks late with my salary payment this month and I'm getting really desperate for the money. I've asked again and again, they always say it's 'tomorrow'. Can anyone suggest what I can do? Zara

Best answer – chosen by Askaboutjobs users

Hi, I know how you feel, I've had the same problem. Here's what I did: I wrote them a letter and gave them a deadline in writing. You could do the same. And say that if you haven't had it by a certain date, you're getting a solicitor involved. It's not as if you're asking for an advance, they're just being unreasonable by withholding money. You can always ring the helpline.

Cheers, Lisa

Post 3:

I've just started an office job. I got my first payslip the other day, and I couldn't believe how much had been deducted. When I asked, they just said it's because the tax code is BR. What's that supposed to mean? I'm worried and don't know what to do.

Ta, Dan

Best answer – chosen by Askaboutjobs users

OK, it's a bit complicated. Basically, the last place you worked should give you a P45 form, showing how much you were taxed. Your new employer then uses this to work out how much tax you have to pay. You've been given a temporary code while they work this out. So you should get it all back in the end. One piece of advice though – hang on to all your payslips, because you might want to contact your local tax office. Your payslips are the best record of how much tax you've paid. Kelly89

PS – check out this site for more info: http://www.direct.gov.uk/en/MoneyTaxAndBenefits/Taxes/BeginnersGuideToTax/IncomeTax/Taxcodes/index.htm

2 People often use these websites to find answers to questions they have. Say which of the posts (with their answers) will help the following people, and why.

a Sri works five and a half hours without a break and wants to know if his employer is breaking the law.
b Rosa wants to know how to find out how much money is deducted from her salary before she is paid.
c Mani has a work problem that he needs to discuss with an expert in private.

3 Which of the people who wrote the replies

a advised the reader to keep relevant paperwork?
b suggested the person should take legal action?
c recommended a helpline?
d pointed out the employer's legal obligations?
e said the employer is breaking the law?

10a Phoning in sick

Type of activity
Listening to a phone call in which an employee phones in sick. Practising the conversation. Pair and group work.

AECC reference
Lr/E3.1c; Sc/E3.4d; Lr/L1.2a; Sc/L1.3d

Aims
To demonstrate common practice for reporting absence through sickness in the UK. To raise awareness of appropriate language for discussing health issues sensitively.

Vocabulary
sick leave, shift, ill, illness

Preparation
Photocopy one worksheet for each learner.

Differentiation
Stronger learners: Give learners copies of the audioscript and ask them to identify instances of polite and sympathetic usage of language.

Weaker learners: Instead of task 5, give pairs of learners a copy of the audioscript and ask them to take the roles of Hasan and Sarah.

Warmer
Elicit common illnesses and symptoms, writing any useful lexis on the board. If appropriate, you could ask students about when they were last ill, and, if they needed to miss college or work, who they informed and how.

1 Give each learner a worksheet. Ask learners to read the extract and discuss the question. Conduct feedback, explaining that different companies have different rules about sick leave.

2 Ask learners to work in pairs to do this task.

> **Answers**
> **a** consecutive **b** self-certify
> **c** absence **d** disqualify

3 (▶16) Tell learners they are going to listen to Hasan phone in sick. Ask them to listen to see if he follows company rules. Play the recording.

> **Answers**
> Yes

4 (▶16) Ask learners to discuss the questions in pairs and try and remember what the speakers said. Play the recording again for learners to check.

> **Answers**
> **1** calling **2** through **3** This is
> **4** I'm afraid I won't be able to **5** cover
> **6** yourself **7** good **8** get well

5 Ask learners whether Hasan explains his absence politely and effectively (he does), and whether Sarah Howard responds in a sympathetic manner (she does). Put learners in pairs and ask them to choose one of these scenarios, and practise similar conversations.

Extension
The audioscript can be exploited in a number of ways:

• Ask learners to find and highlight phrases in the audioscript connected with health and illness (*a splitting headache; be off sick*)

• Help the learners to identify multi-word verbs and strong collocations, and these chunks can then be analysed for their stress pattern (*go DOWN with something; SICK note*), using the recording if necessary.

You could conduct a whole-class discussion comparing absence from work procedure and legislation with that in the candidates' own countries. Some students may express surprise that employees are entitled to self-certify for up to one week. However, it may be worth pointing out that employers do keep records of employees' sickness absence, and that this information can be given to possible future employers.

Links to other themes in this book
For more on telephoning, see 7c and 14a. For more on talking with a manager, see 8b and 9b.

> **Answers: Self-study exercises**
>
> **1** 1 b 2 b 3 a 4 a 5 a 6 b 7 b 8 b
>
> **2** surname not in block caps; small 'p' used for Peters; time and date the wrong way round; inconsistent ways used to write dates (though only 'March 2 Tues' is incorrect); 's' missing from '2 days'

Phoning in sick 10a

1 Read the extract on sick leave from Thorntons' company policy. Are the rules at Thorntons the same as in your workplace?

SICK LEAVE

If you are too ill to come to work, you must inform your line manager at least two hours before starting your shift on your first day of absence.

If you are ill for more than five consecutive days, you need a doctor's note that explains your absence.

If you are ill for five or fewer days, you may self-certify.

Failure to comply with these rules may disqualify the employee from receiving sick pay.

2 Which word from the extract

a describes things that follow each other without interruption?
b means that you can confirm to your employer that you are ill, and don't need a note from a doctor?
c means being away from work?
d means not being allowed to do or have something?

Hasan works at the warehouse of Thorntons, a large furniture shop. Today he feels very ill, and phones his line manager, Sarah Howard.

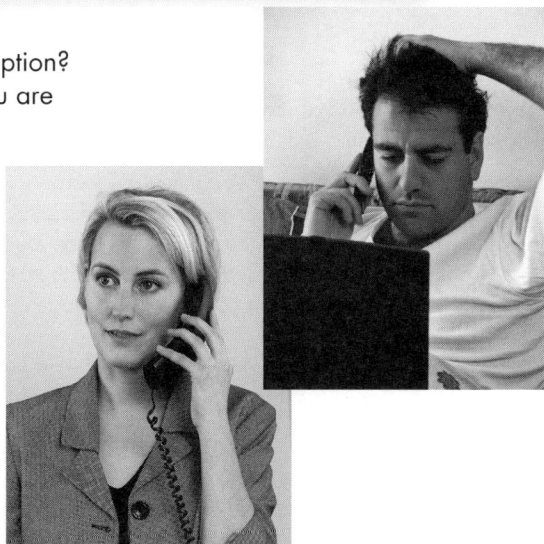

3 Listen to their conversation. Does he follow the company rules?

4 Look at the sentences from the conversation. What did the speakers say?

1 Who's _calling / talking_, please?

2 Just putting you _across / through_ now.

3 _I am / This is_ Hasan speaking.

4 _I'm afraid I won't be able to / I can't_ come in.

5 I'm sure we can get someone to _cover / put on_ your shift.

6 So you can say that you don't consider _yourself / you_ fit to work.

7 Thank you for letting me know in _early / good_ time.

8 _Get well / Come back to work_ soon.

5 Work with a partner. One of you is the employee, and the other is their manager. Practise similar conversations using the following information. Use some of the phrases from task 3.

Problem: severe backache **Extra info:** probably hurt it carrying shopping yesterday	**Problem:** personal (you'd rather not discuss it) **Extra info:** hospital appointment today	**Problem:** child has flu **Extra info:** still trying to get doctor's appointment

From *English at Work* © Cambridge University Press 2011 **PHOTOCOPIABLE** 65

10b Dealing with customer complaints

Type of activity
Listening to phone messages; reading and analysing emails; writing an email. Individual, pair and group work.

AECC reference
Lr/E3.3b; Ww/E3.1a; Lr/L1.1a; Wt/L1.4a

Aims
To develop students' listening, note-taking and email writing skills.

Vocabulary
delivery, delay, overcharge, deliver, unsatisfactory, debit an account, misunderstanding, timber, ruined

Preparation
Photocopy one worksheet for each learner.

Differentiation
Stronger learners: draw their attention to some of the higher-level language not focused on in the self-study exercises: *rest assured, redeem*. You could ask them to infer the meaning of these words from context.

Weaker learners: underline the phrases in the emails which are the answers to task 4, so that learners can find them more easily.

Warmer
Ask learners what kind of complaints customers make most often, and how these are dealt with in their place of work.

1 (▶17) Give each learner a worksheet. Ask learners to read the list of common complaints and make sure everyone understands what they mean. Tell them you are going to play two recorded messages. Ask them to identify which two of the four complaints are made in the messages.

Answers
1 b **2** c

2 (▶17) Ask learners to work alone to write the description of each complaint on the message notes. Play the recording again and ask learners to check their answers in pairs.

Answers
1 Mr Sharma, 774422 , b **2** Sam Harris, 07737 298 107 or harris@aecconstruction.co.uk, c

3 Ask learners how they feel staff at Thomsons should respond. Ask learners to read the two emails and identify which complaint it is a response to, and write the appropriate name in the email.

Answers
Email 1 Mr Harris   Email 2 Mr Sharma

4 Ask learners to work in pairs to do this task.

Answers
a offer my sincere apologies
b With regard to your phone message / Further to your voicemail
c concerned to learn
d by the close of business today
e your continuing custom
f prioritise
g resolve this issue
h as a gesture of goodwill
i It now appears

5 (▶18) Make sure learners know the meaning of the word *timber*. Ask them to write a phone message memo similar to those in task 2. Play the recording.

Answers
Anna Hart called
Timber delivered but has got wet and is ruined
Contact by email: hart@nowmail.co.uk

6 Ask learners to work in groups to draft an email reply. Encourage them to use some of the language featured on the worksheet.

Extension
If appropriate, learners could send their replies to you by email, and you could reply with corrections or suggestions.

Links to other themes in this book
For more on formal writing/emailing, see 2c, 15a and 16a.

Answers: Self-study exercises

1 1 regard   2 sincere   3 concerned   4 resolve   5 custom   6 goodwill   7 error

Dealing with customer complaints

Thomsons Building Supplies is a retailer providing building materials to a wide range of private and trade customers.

1 Listen to the voicemail messages from Thomsons' customers. Which complaint (a–d) is each customer making? There are two options which you do not need.

a a delivery has been delayed.
b a customer has been overcharged.
c the wrong items have been delivered.
d the quality of the goods is unsatisfactory.

2 Listen again and complete the phone message memos with the caller's name, contact details and the complaint (a, b, c, or d).

> Caller 1
> Name:
> Complaint:
> Contact details:

> Caller 2
> Name:
> Complaint:
> Contact details:

3 Later in the day, staff at Thomsons wrote to the two callers. Read the emails and write the surnames in the right places.

Email 1

To:
From: Kasia Kwiatkowska

Dear ....,

With regard to your phone message, I was concerned to learn about the error in your order. It now appears that your order was mixed up with another customer's. We are currently working to resolve this issue, and will prioritise your order to make sure it is with you by the close of business today.

I will try to contact you on your mobile again this afternoon.

With apologies once again,

Kasia Kwiatkowska
Customer Services Manager
Thomsons Building Supplies

Email 2

To:
From: Joanne Thomson

Dear ....,

Further to your voicemail, I would like to offer my sincere apologies for the error in processing your payment. The amount of £656.23 has been refunded to your account.

In addition, as a gesture of goodwill, a credit note to the value of £50 has been added to your account, which you are free to redeem on your next purchase from Thomsons Building Supplies.

Please accept my apologies for any inconvenience this has caused, and we look forward to your continuing custom.

With best wishes,

Joanne Thomson
Managing Director
Thomsons Building Supplies

4 The emails contain a lot of useful language for discussing problems. Find words and phrases from the emails which mean:

a say I am very sorry
b about your message (x 2)
c sorry to hear
d before the end of the day
e doing more business with you
f deal with something first
g solve the problem
h in order to make it up to you
i We've just found out

5 Listen to another recorded message where the customer complains about the quality of the timber delivered. Write a phone message memo like those in task 2.

> Name:
> Complaint:
> Contact details:

6 Write an email reply to the caller in task 5, using some of the phrases from task 4.

10c Everyday problems

Type of activity
Reading a blog and focusing on problem-related vocabulary. Group and individual work.

AECC reference
Rw/E3.5a; Rt/E3.4a; Rt/L1.5a; Rw/L1.3a

Aims
To present problem-related vocabulary in context, and encourage learners to use context to work out meaning.

Vocabulary
stuck, call something off, reschedule

Preparation
Photocopy one worksheet for each learner.

Differentiation
Stronger learners: ask them to analyse the blog in task 2 for typical features of informal writing.

Weaker learners: allow use of dictionaries for task 5.

Warmer

Ask learners if they have heard of Murphy's law. Explain that this is a phrase people say when lots of things go wrong. Explain that people say that Murphy's law is 'Anything that can go wrong, will go wrong.' Ask them if they can give any examples.

1 Discuss the picture as a class. Elicit and write on the board the problems at work that the learners report.

2 Ask the learners to skim read the blog to answer the question and then compare answers with a partner.

> **Suggested answers**
> Sebastian has 11 problems, but it does not matter if learners find slightly more or slightly fewer. The 11 are: got stuck in rush hour; couldn't find a parking place; lift not working; loads of deadlines; late for work; computer died; couldn't print anything; photocopier jammed; double-booked appointments; colleague couldn't stand in; forgot about playing squash.

3 Draw learners' attention to the highlighted words. Ask them to work in pairs and match them to the definitions.

> **Answers**
>
> **a** up and runnning **b** overheated **c** schedule
> **d** snag **e** deadlines **f** jammed
> **g** stand in (for sb)

4 Ask learners to do this task alone, and then check answers with a partner.

> **Answers**
>
> **1** appointment **2** computer **3** lift **4** traffic
> **5** deadline **6** squash game **7** paper
> **8** meetings

5 Ask learners to use context to try and work out the meanings of the words and phrases in italics.

> **Answers**
>
> **1** double-booked = have two things arranged for the same time
> **2** crashed = stopped working
> **3** out of order = not working
> **4** held up = delayed
> **5** push back = postpone
> **6** It slipped my mind. = I forgot about it.
> **7** run out of = use the last one of something, so that there are none left.
> **8** clash = be planned for the same time, in a way that is inconvenient

Extension
You could refer the learners to *www.dictionary.cambridge.org*, where the *Cambridge Advanced Learner's Dictionary* can be accessed, and encourage them to find examples of how the words from this activity are used. You could make the activity more challenging by asking learners to also find an 'authentic' example of the word in use by typing it into a search engine.

> **Answers: Self-study exercises**
>
> **1** 1 ~~run off~~ run out 2 ~~off order~~ out of order
>   3 ✓   4 ~~I slipped~~ It slipped 5 ✓
>   6 ~~stand out for~~ stand in for   7 ✓

1 Look at the cartoon. Have you ever felt the same way?

2 Read Sebastian's blog. How many problems has Sebastian had today?

---

sebastiansworkblog.com

Oh dear – you can't believe the day I've had at work today!!!!!!!!!!!!!!!

Got stuck in the rush hour on the way in to work, then couldn't get a parking space – typical!!!!!!

Then guess what – lift not working!!! Great when you work on the sixth floor. So by this time I figured it was gonna be one of those days with just one <u>snag</u> after another… So here I was at my desk with loads of <u>deadlines</u> for things that need to be finished urgently, + already late for work. Oh well, at least there was no shortage of coffee – you really need it sometimes!

And then of course my computer died, but at least the IT guys were able to get it <u>up and running</u> again pretty quickly. Couldn't print anything though could I? Someone had used the last paper, and not replaced it. Great!!! Then it was the photocopier's turn – had to get <u>jammed</u> didn't it? I was making a couple of hundred copies, but it <u>overheated</u> inside… aaaaargh!

And as if all that wasn't bad enough… I checked my <u>schedule</u> cos I knew I had a couple of appointments in the afternoon, and guess what: two meetings with different clients, but here's the catch: both booked for exactly the same time – in completely different places, of course!!! Typical! Tried to get a colleague to <u>stand in for</u> me at the last minute, but she couldn't and had to go home early, so had to call one of them off.

And then to cap it all – I was supposed to be playing squash with my mate at the end of the day. Only I was so exhausted that I forgot all about it. Whoops! Oh well, at least it's Friday tomorrow!

---

3 Match the underlined words and phrases from the blog with the definitions.

a (describing a machine) working properly, especially after it has been broken
b became too hot
c list of planned activities showing the times or dates when they will happen
d a small problem
e times by which work must be completed
f blocked and not working, because paper is stuck in it
g to take the place of another person at an event, because they cannot be there

4 Use the words in the box to complete the things Sebastian said during the day to his colleagues. (You do not need to use them all.)

lift	traffic	car	office	deadline	computer	squash game	paper	appointment	meetings

1 We seem to have *run out of* ……………… – do you know where I can get some more?

2 Would you be able to give me a hand with my ………………? It seems to have *crashed*.

3 It looks as if the ……………… is *out of order*. Oh well, the exercise'll do me good!

4 I'm really sorry I'm late – I got *held up* in ……………… .

5 Could we *push* this ……………… *back* to next week? I'm afraid I don't think I can finish it today.

6 Look, I've got two ……………… that *clash*. Any chance you could attend one of them for me?

7 I must apologise, but I'm afraid I'm *double-booked*. Do you mind if we reschedule our ……………… until next week?

8 Oh look, yeah, of course, the ……………… after work. It completely *slipped my mind*. I'm really sorry.

5 Can you work out what the words and phrases in italics mean?

11a What's the law?

Type of activity
Discussion; listening to radio interview. Individual and pair work.

AECC reference
Lr/E3.2a; Rw/E3.1a; Lr/1.2a

Aims
To develop learners' speaking and listening skills.

Vocabulary
lawyer, legislation, obligation, contract, paperwork, bank holiday, ban, average, break the law

Preparation
Photocopy one worksheet for learner. You may want to find out more about the legal terms presented in this activity by looking at www.direct.gov.uk/en/Employment/Employees/index.htm

You may also wish to check that the information contained in this unit is still up-to-date.

Differentiation
Stronger learners: before the listening, you could ask them to explain what they think the phrases in the box (task 4) might mean.

Weaker learners: fill in some of the answers on the grid for tasks 3 for them if you feel the listening load and writing load may be too demanding for them.

Warmer
To introduce learners to the topic, ask them questions such as:

- How many days' leave do you have a year?
- Do you work on Bank Holidays?

Tell the learners they are going to be introduced to some of the main employment laws in the UK.

1 Give each learner a worksheet. Put learners in pairs to discuss the cartoon.

2 Ask learners to discuss the statements in pairs. Encourage them to discuss whether they think the statements are true or false, but not to write this on their worksheets. Explain that you do not expect them to know the right answers. Do not check answers until after task 3.

3 (▶19) Explain that the learners are going to hear part of a radio programme in which an employment lawyer is talking about the same issues. Ask learners to put a tick in the second column next to those statements that are true. Play the recording.

> **Answers**
> **a** T **b** F **c** T **d** F **e** F

4 Ask learners if they can remember which of the phrases in the box were used in connection with which statements in task 3. Do not check answers until after task 5.

5 (▶19) Play the recording again for learners to check.

> **Answers**
> **a** National Minimum Wage
> **b** legally binding; verbal offer of work
> **c** statutory holiday
> **d** overtime
> **e** nightshift; broken the law

6 Ask learners to choose the correct option.

> **Answers**
> **a** Can **b** have to **c** obligation **d** entitled to
> **e** obliged **f** advisable **g** ban **h** enforced

7 Encourage learners to compare the UK laws with those of their own country. If they do not know what the law stipulates in their country, ask them whether they feel the laws are appropriate, or if they should be changed.

Extension
Ask learners to research these aspects of employment legislation online, and check if they are still up-to-date. and to report back to the class. The Directgov website is recommended: www.direct.gov.uk/en/Employment/Employees/index.htm

Links to other themes in this book
For more on equal opportunities, see 8. For more on Employment law, see 5a and 8a.

> ## Answers: Self-study exercises
>
> **1** 1 Sex Discrimination Act
> 2 Race Relations Act
> 3 Equal Pay Act
> 4 Disability Discrimination Act
> 5 Statutory Maternity Pay Regulations
> 6 Human Rights Act 1998

1 Look at the cartoons. Who are the people? How are they feeling? Why?

2 Look at the following statements and discuss them with a partner. Do you think they are true or false?

Statements	True?	Phrases
a There are laws about how much employees must be paid.		
b No employment contract exists if the employee has received nothing in writing.		
c All full-time workers can have at least 28 days, leave per year.		
d Everybody who works on a bank holiday will be paid extra.		
e Night workers cannot work more than eight hours in a 24-hour period.		

3 Now listen to an employment lawyer talking on a radio programme. Are the statements true or false?

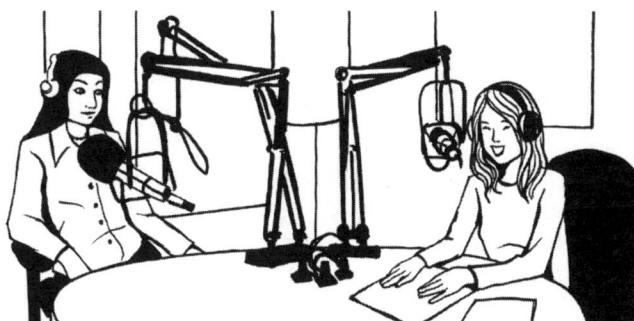

4 Look at the following phrases which were used during the conversation. Which statement (a–e) from task 2 are they connected with? Write them in the *Phrases* column in task 2.

> overtime   statutory holiday   nightshift   National Minimum Wage
> legally binding   broken the law   verbal offer of work

5 Listen again and check.

6 Talking about legal requirements. What did the speakers say? Choose the correct answer.

a *Can / Shall* employers pay staff as much or as little as they want?
b Now this is the National Minimum Wage, isn't it – do employers *must / have to* stick to that?
c … in the past it was just a guideline, but it is now a legal *recommendation / obligation*.
d Well everyone is *forbidden / entitled to* statutory holiday of 28 days a year.
e … the employer isn't *advised / obliged* to pay a higher rate for that …
f Obviously it would be *advisable / legal* for both sides to get everything in writing–
g I've heard there's a *ban / obligation* on them working nightshifts longer than eight hours …
h … but is that actually *obliged / enforced*, do you think?

7 Discussion

Are the statements from task 2 true or false in your country? How are the laws different from those of the UK?

11b Annual leave

Type of activity
Role play. Individual and group work.

AECC reference
Sd/E3.1f; Sd/E3.1g; Lr/L1.2b; Sd/L1.3a

Aims
To give learners practice at taking part in a spoken negotiation.

Vocabulary
estate agency, a first come first served basis, get first shout, make do with, clash, prioritise, entitlement, overseas, alternate

Preparation
Photocopy one worksheet for each learner. Cut the worksheet up as indicated, reserving the cards at the bottom for task 3.

Differentiation
Stronger learners: group them together and encourage them to invent other holiday requests and needs.

Weaker learners: group them together for task 2 to give them optimum chance to speak.

Warmer
Ask learners who work how much leave they have every year, and what they need to do to arrange when they can take this leave. Ask if they have ever had any problems doing this.

1 Ask learners to read the email and answer the questions with a partner.

> **Answers**
> **a** He wants to make it fairer.
> **b** Discuss with colleagues when they want time off, and tell him once they have agreed.

2 Put learners in groups of four. Explain that each group is one of the teams at Fastmove and that they should negotiate their holidays as requested by their director. Read through the suggested phrases with them and elicit other phrases they could use. Encourage them to use these during the discussion. Remind them that a maximum of one person can be away at any one time, and that each has 20 days' leave. Finally, give each learner a role card and monitor the discussions.

Extension
Learners could write an email reply to Mr Solariego summarising what their group has agreed, and requesting leave on the dates they require.

Answers: Self-study exercises

1 1 d 2 c 3 b 4 a

2 1 clash 2 entitlement 3 make do with
   4 prioritise

1 Moveready is a London estate agency. Read the email from the manager, Mr Solariego, and answer the questions:

a Why has he decided to organise staff annual leave differently this year?

b What does he want staff to do?

To: All staff

From: Javier.Solariego (mail to managingdirector@moveready.co.uk)

Subject: IMPORTANT – new arrangements for annual leave

Hello folks,

I'm trying to arrange everybody's annual leave at the moment. As you know, in the past we have run this on a first-come, first-served basis. However, this has meant that the same people get first shout at the most popular times, which are of course school holidays and half terms, as well as Christmas and New Year. This means that others have to make do with whatever is left over, which doesn't always seem fair.

That's why I've decided to make a change this year. I'd like you to discuss with your colleagues in your team when you would each like to take your leave, and then let me know what you decide. Please remember, though, that we cannot have more than one member of any team away from work at the same time. You'll need to plan your leave so that there are no clashes with your colleagues.

So could I ask you to prioritise this, and get back to me with your leave requests by the end of the week by replying to this email? With thanks,

Javier Solariego

Managing Director

---

2 Work in groups of four. You are in the lettings team at Moveready. Have a meeting to arrange when you can all take your 20 days of annual leave.

You could use the following phrases.

- I was hoping to …
- Wouldn't it be fairer if …?
- That would clash with …
- I was wondering if I would be able to …
- in order to avoid a clash …

- That's not ideal – you see, I'm hoping to …
- Is there any other time you could take off?
- [x] days of my annual leave entitlement remaining
- if possible
- If I can …, then you would be able to …

Role cards for task 2

Student 1

You usually go abroad for two weeks to visit your family at Christmas and New Year, and would like to again this year. Your children are overseas, and you don't see them very often.

You'd also like some time off in the school summer holidays.

Student 3

You want to take four weeks' leave as soon as possible so you can go on a long holiday. You don't mind when this is. If it's during school term-time you'd be happy, as air fares are likely to be cheaper then.

Help your colleagues negotiate their time off.

Student 2

You have worked over the Christmas and New Year period in the last three years, and would like to have some time off then to relax in front of the TV. Last year, you and Student 4 agreed that the two of you would take it in turns to have Christmas off, starting this year.

You'd like some time off at half term or in the school summer holidays.

Student 4

Last year, you made an agreement with Student 2, who agreed to work over Christmas so that you could go away (which you did). You also agreed to work on alternate Christmases, but you're not sure if Student 2 remembers this informal arrangement. You'd like to spend Christmas with your new baby.

You'd also like some time off at half term.

11c Maternity and paternity leave

Type of activity
Reading and discussing an information text. Individual and group work.

AECC reference
Sd/E3.1d; Rt/E3.4a; Sd/L1.2a; Rt/L1.5a

Aims
To develop learners' reading skills, vocabulary and knowledge of UK workplace practices.

Vocabulary
apply for, entitled to, purpose, regardless of, detriment, employment tribunal, notify

Preparation
Photocopy one worksheet for each learner.

Differentiation
If any learners are current or expectant parents, they are likely to know more about parental leave. In order to exploit the potential for peer teaching, try to group parents with non-parents.

Warmer
If appropriate, find out how many of the learners are parents. Ask how easy they think it is to be a parent and to have a job at the same time. Explain that they are going to find out about the law regarding pay and time off for new parents.

1 Give each learner a worksheet. Ask learners to work in pairs and match the definitions.

> **Answers**
> 1 b 2 c 3 d 4 a

2 Put learners in small groups to discuss these questions. Encourage learners to talk about what they think the answers are or should be. Set a time limit for the discussion. Do not check answers until after task 4.

3 Ask learners to look at the text, and quickly decide who it was written for.

> **Answers**
> Although useful for everyone, it was mainly written for employers.

Ask learners to read the text and match the headings. Ask them to check their answers in pairs

> **Answers**
> 1 a 2 c 3 f 4 i 5 h 6 e 7 g
> 8 d 9 b

Extension
Ask learners to do some online research, and find out more about other employee entitlements, e.g. sick pay, sick leave. They could find out what policies their employer has, or use the directgov website to find out more about UK law.

Links to other themes in this book
For more on Employment law, see 5a and 8a. For more on pay, see 9b and 9c.

> ### Answers: Self-study exercises
>
> **1** 1 paying 2 take 3 suffered 4 took 5 get
> 6 gave
>
> **2** 1 for 2 under 3 of 4 from 5 of 6 from

Maternity and paternity leave (11c)

1 Match the definitions.

1	paternity	a	decided or controlled by law
2	maternity	b	the state of being a father
3	maternity leave	c	related to pregnancy and birth
4	statutory	d	a period in which a woman is legally allowed to be absent from work in the weeks before and after she gives birth

2 In groups, talk about the questions, and try to guess the answers.

a Who has the right to take maternity leave?
b When does a man need to apply for paternity leave?
c What is parental leave for?
d Can a man get time off work when his child is born?
e When does a woman get Statutory Maternity Pay (SMP)?
f Who actually pays the maternity and paternity pay?
g Can people on maternity leave still lose their job?
h What happens if a woman has more than one baby – can she take longer maternity leave?
i Do pregnant women actually have to take maternity leave?

3 Read the information from a government website about maternity and paternity leave and pay. Match the questions (a–i) from task 2 with the paragraphs (1–9) below.

When an employee becomes a parent – maternity and paternity leave

1 _____

All pregnant employees, i.e. those working under a contract of employment, are entitled to take up to 52 weeks' Statutory Maternity Leave (SML) around the birth of their child. It does not matter how long the employee has worked for you to qualify.

2 _____

The purpose of maternity leave is to allow the mother to give birth and to recover from giving birth. Maternity and paternity leave are for the parents to bond with and care for the new child.

3 _____

You, as the employer, need to pay this. However, you should be able to recover most of this money from the government as long as the employee was paying secondary Class 1 National Insurance contributions.

4 _____

An employee must take a minimum of two weeks' leave after the birth of her child – or four weeks if she works in a factory.

5 _____

SML remains at 52 weeks regardless of the number of children resulting from a single pregnancy.

6 _____

SMP is payable when the employee is not at work because of her pregnancy or because she has given birth. It is paid for 39 weeks – usually the first 39 weeks of maternity leave.

7 _____

Employees are protected from suffering a detriment or dismissal for taking, or seeking to take, maternity leave. If an employee believes you have treated them detrimentally under these circumstances, she can take a claim of sex discrimination to an employment tribunal.

8 _____

An employee qualifies for Statutory Paternity Leave (SPL) on the birth of a baby if he:
• will have responsibility for the baby's upbringing
• is the biological father of the baby and/or the mother's husband or partner.

9 _____

The rules for the father are the same as for the mother: he must notify you 15 weeks before the expected week of childbirth.

12a Helping out

Type of activity
Listening to dialogues. Individual and pair work.

AECC reference
Lr/E3.1c; Lr/3.7d; Lr/L1.1a; Lr/L1.6d

Aims
To familiarise learners with a range of strategies for dealing politely and helpfully with members of the public.

Vocabulary
aslie, customer, visiting tours, ward

Preparation
Photocopy one worksheet for each learner. In addition, photocopy one copy of the audioscript (track 2, p. 126–7) for each learner.

Differentiation
Stronger learners: for task 8, encourage them to learn some of their lines in the dialogue so that they can perform from memory.

Weaker learners: for task 8, ask learners to act out one of the dialogues on the worksheet rather than writing their own.

Warmer
Write the following questions on the board for learners to ask each other in small groups.

- When did you last ask someone at work for help?
- When did you last help someone to do something?

1 Give each learner a worksheet. Elicit the names of the places in the pictures (a hospital, a bus stop, a supermarket, a café).

2 (▶20) Explain that learners are going to hear three conversations. Ask them to identify where the conversations take place. Play the recording.

> **Answers**
> **1** d **2** e **3** b

3 (▶20) Ask learners to listen for the phrases in the three conversations. Play the recording again.

> **Answers**
> **Conversation 1** I can't seem to   Could you just tell me where they are?   I'm here to help. Much appreciated.
>
> **Conversation 2** I was wondering if I could Would that be OK?   I'm afraid the thing is So the answer's going to have to be no, I'm afraid.
>
> **Conversation 3** Sorry, can I just ask you something?   Is this something you can help me with?   What you want to do is   That's very kind of you.

4 Ask the learners to think about the meanings of the phrases, and write them in the appropriate box.

> **Answers**
> TO ASK FOR HELP   I was wondering if you could   Would that be OK?   I can't seem to Sorry, can I just ask you something?
> Could you tell me where they are?
> Is this something you can help me with?
>
> TO HELP   What you want to do is   I'm here to help.
> TO SAY 'THANK YOU'   That's very kind of you. Much appreciated.
> TO SAY YOU CAN'T HELP   I'm afraid the thing is So the answer's going to have to be no, I'm afraid.

5 Ask learners to discuss these questions in pairs. Check answers and explain that 'just' is often used to soften request or instructions.

> **Answers**
> **a** 2 sounds more polite   **b** 2 sounds friendlier

6 (▶20) Explain that the word *just* is missing from the conversation in four places. Ask learners to work in pairs to say where *just* should go. Then play the recording, pausing after each *just*. Note that *just* could fit in other places in the conversation.

> **Answers**
> See audioscript (track 20, p. 126–7)

7 Give each learner a copy of the audioscript (track 20, p126–7). Ask learners to underline the word *sorry* each time it occurs in the three conversations. Ask them to decide why it is being used in each case.

> **Answers**
> Conversation 1: *Sorry, do you have a second?* = 2
> Conversation 2: *Sorry, but I'm afraid the thing is …* = 3
> Conversation 3: *Sorry, can I just ask you something?* = 2; *Sorry, won't be a minute* = 1

8 Put learners in pairs, and ask them to write, rehearse and act out a dialogue using some of the language they have learnt.

Extension
Ask learners to notice the next time they hear a colleague use the words 'sorry' and 'just' (outside class) and be ready to briefly report back on their findings in the next class.

Links to other themes in this book
For more on customer service, see unit 14.

> ### Answers: Self-study exercises
>
> **1** ~~can just~~ can I just; ~~how I~~ how can I; ~~seem find~~ seem to find; ~~do go~~ do is go; ~~you showing~~ you mind showing; ~~you to follow~~ you like to follow; ~~kind you~~ kind of you; ~~we're to help~~ we're here to help; ~~Appreciated.~~ Much appreciated.

1 Look at the pictures. Where are these places?

a

b

c

d

2 Listen to three conversations in some of the places above. Which places are they?

3 Listen again. In which conversation were the following phrases used?

Much appreciated.   So the answer's going to have to be no, I'm afraid.   I'm afraid the thing is I was wondering if you could   Would that be OK?   That's very kind of you.   I can't seem to Sorry, can I just ask you something?   Could you just tell me where they are? What you want to do is   Is this something you can help me with?   I'm here to help.

4 Why did the speakers use the phrases from task 3? Write the phrases under the correct heading.

TO ASK FOR HELP	TO HELP
TO SAY 'THANK YOU'	TO SAY YOU CAN'T HELP

5 Listen to and look at the pairs of sentences, and answer the questions.

a Which one sounds more polite?
　1 *Can I ask you a question?*
　2 *Can I just ask you a question?*

b Which one sounds friendlier?
　1 *I'll have a look for you.*
　2 *I'll just have a look for you.*

6 Read conversation 1. The word *just* has been deleted. Can you identify the three times the speakers use *just*? Now listen and check.

A: Sorry, do you have a second?

B: Yes, how can I help?

A: I can't seem to find the biscuits.

B: Right, well do you mean chocolate biscuits?

A: No, you know, savoury biscuits, crackers, for having with cheese, not the chocolate ones. Could you tell me where they are?

B: Yeah, I'm here to help. You want aisle six.

A: Aisle six?

B: Yeah, you're quite close, actually. You see where it says pasta, there?

A: Yeah.

B: Well, next to that basically.

A: Oh yeah, right, I see. Thanks. Much appreciated.

7 Look at the three conversations. Underline the word *sorry* in the three conversations. In each case, decide why the person says sorry. Is it

1 to apologise for a delay?
2 as a way of saying 'excuse me'?
3 to introduce news that someone doesn't want to hear?

12b A green workplace

Type of activity
Reading a web article; listening to two colleagues discussing the article; discussion. Individual and pair work.

AECC reference
Rt/E3.7a; Lr/E3.1b; Lr/L1.6a; Rt/L1.5a

Aims
To develop learners' reading, listening and speaking skills.

Vocabulary
thermostat, chuck, commute, unplug, ink, economical, green, frugal, get rid of, on standby, regulate

Preparation
Photocopy one worksheet for each learner. Additionally, you may wish to copy the audioscript (track 21, p. 127) for task 7.

Differentiation
Stronger learners: omit task 5 and make task 6 the first listening task.

Weaker learners: make a copy of the audioscript for learners who find listening more challenging.

Warmer
Ask learners what 'being green' means in terms of the environment. Put them in pairs and ask them to find out from their partner one thing they do that is green, and one thing that isn't.

1 Give each learner a worksheet. Ask learners to work in pairs and discuss the environmental impact of the things shown in the pictures.

2 Ask learners to look at the article and do this task. Set a time limit of 30 seconds for this.

> **Answers**
> to encourage readers to make their workplace and work habits more environmentally friendly

3 Ask learners to do this task alone. Again set a time limit (one minute).

> **Answers**
> **1** b **2** e **3** f **4** g **5** a **6** c **7** d

4 Ask learners to read the article in more detail to answer this question and allow more time accordingly.

> **Answers**
> all except step 2

5 (▶21) Tell the learners that they are going to listen to two architects discussing the suggestions in the article. Play the recording and discuss the answers as a whole class.

> **Answers**
> They discuss the steps in the following order:
> 6, 1, 7, 5, 3, 2, 4

6 (▶21) Play the recording again and ask learners to discuss their answers in pairs.

> **Answers**
> a 1 and 5
>
> b 6 (they say they don't do more than they need to), 3 (they just open the window), 2 (they don't see the point), 7 (too expensive / false economy), 4 (impractical)

7 (▶21) Ask learners to work in pairs to do this task. Check answers by playing the recording again, and stopping after each phrase is used, or give learners a copy of the audioscript.

> **Answers**
> **1** printer **2** printer **3** cups **4** turning off lights and equipment **5** printer **6** replacing pcs with laptops **7** lights **8** plants **9** telecommuting **10** computers **11** lights **12** telecommuting

Extension
Ask learners to write an email to their manager or work colleagues, suggesting steps they could take to make their workplace greener, using some of the language from this unit.

Answers: Self-study exercises

1 1 kettle 2 mistake 3 to plug 4 to dispose
5 recycling

2 1 disposable cup
2 fake greenery
3 disposable razor
4 unplug the computer
5 chuck / throw it in the bin
6 coffee time

1 Look at the pictures. Do you associate these things with wasting energy or saving energy?

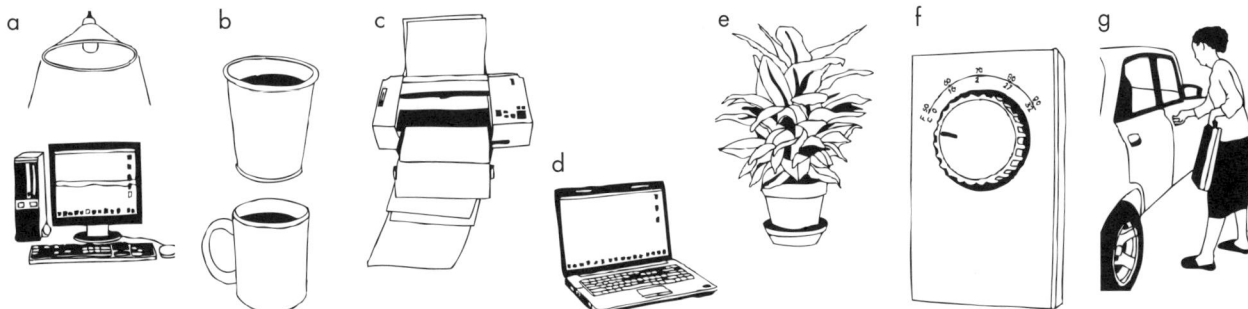

a   b   c   d   e   f   g

2 Look at the article from a website. What is the purpose of the article?

3 Match a picture from task 1 with a paragraph from the article.

4 According to the article, which of the seven steps can save you money?

Green living, green working?

Whether you work in a home office of one or a corporate complex with thousands of employees, consider these steps to reduce your business's impact on the environment:

1. Start a bring-your-own coffee mug policy for the break room and ditch the foam cups. Your company will reduce waste and save cash as well.

2. Bring real plants into the office. Fake greenery might be low maintenance, but the real thing adds beauty and oxygen to your surroundings. This is a way in which you can offset some of the emissions from all your energy-hungry office equipment.

3. Re-programme the thermostat. Each degree warmer you leave the thermostat in summer, and each degree cooler you set it in the winter can knock 6 to 8 per cent off energy costs. If it's a warm day outside, but you're cold inside, then you're effectively just chucking energy in the bin!

4. Look into working from home. Every commute not taken saves on time and fuel, not to mention all those fares. Plus, studies have found that telecommuting boosts productivity too. Another option is a four-day week, so instead of being in the office for eight hours five times a week, you're in for ten hours four times a week.

5. Turn off any lights or equipment that don't need to be on when you're not in the office, and – if possible – unplug them too. Every computer left on standby overnight eats up electricity and costs your company money.

6. Watch the paper and ink. Avoid the extravagance of printing documents that could just as easily be emailed, and print necessary papers on both sides. It also helps to institute a recycling programme, and to switch to recycled paper and water-based inks.

7. Consider replacing ageing desktop computers with laptops instead, which are much more economical.

5 Listen to two partners in an architects' firm discussing the article.

What order do they discuss the steps in?

6 Listen again and answer the questions.

a Which of the steps are they going to try?
b Which steps are they not going to try? Why not?

7 Look at the phrases the speakers used. Can you say which of the things from task 2 the speakers were talking about when they used the following.

1 print something off ....
2 double-sided ....
3 disposable ....
4 nag each other ....
5 frugal ....
6 false economy ....

7 stay on ....
8 can't see the point of ....
9 carbon footprint ....
10 on standby ....
11 economise ....
12 get your money's worth ....

12c Working outdoors

Type of activity
Reading an article; matching headings to paragraphs.
Individual work.

AECC reference
Rt/E3.4a; Rw/E3/5a; Rt/L1.5a; Rw/L1.2a

Aims
To develop learners' ability to determine text purpose; to
give practice in reading for detail.

Vocabulary
*release, fresh air, change of scenery, agricultural,
construction, entertain, client, waiting staff, activity,
demand, uniform, vest*

Preparation
Photocopy one worksheet for each learner. In addition,
you may want to make extra copies and cut them up for
your learners (see note on Differentiation below).

Differentiation
Weaker learners: for task 2, work closely with them,
helping them to pick out the text words that are related
to the jobs.

Stronger learners: ask them to do task 2 without
referring to the list of jobs in order to make it more
challenging.

Warmer
Tell the learners that you are going to list several jobs
which have something in common; learners' task is to work
out what they have in common. Your list could include the
following: fireman, agricultural labourer, site engineer,
police officer, motorcycle courier, roofer, gardener,
professional footballer. Answer: they all work outside. Ask
the learners if they have ever worked outside, and what the
advantages and disadvantages are.

1 Give each learner a worksheet. Ask learners to read
the first paragraph and discuss their answer with a
partner.

> **Answers**
> c

2 Ask learners to read the text and match the
paragraphs with the jobs, writing the jobs in the
spaces provided.

> **Answers**
> **1** Agricultural workers **2** Construction workers
> **3** Events managers **4** Catering staff
> **5** Activity co-ordinators **6** Traffic wardens

3 Ask learners to read the text again and answer the
questions. Point out that each question has more than
one answer.

> **Answers**
> **a** agricultural workers, catering staff
> **b** traffic wardens, construction workers
> **c** events managers, catering staff, activity
>   coordinators
> **d** agricultural workers, activity coordinators, traffic
>   wardens

4 Ask learners to work in pairs to find the phrases.

> **Answers**
> **a** physical work
> **b** braving the elements
> **c** office-based role
> **d** rushed off your feet
> **e** make a living
> **f** keep your cool

Extension
Learners talk to a partner, and find out which of these
jobs he or she would most and least like to do, and why.

Answers: Self-study exercises

1 building site; potential employer; high-viz vest;
champagne lunch; breach of motoring law

2 1 champagne lunch   2 potential employer
3 building site   4 high-viz vest
5 breach of motoring law

1 Read the first paragraph of the text. Why has the writer written the text?

a to explain how he chose his job

b to describe his experiences working out of doors

c to persuade readers to consider applying for outdoor jobs

A change of scene?

Have you ever sat in your workplace and stared out of the window, longing to be released from your desk? No matter how nice your workplace is, the same four walls can get a bit much at times and there are many benefits to spending time outside. Many professions can add fresh air to their list of employee benefits, so if you're looking for a change of scenery, here are a few sectors you should consider:

1 _____ Where would we be without all those hard-working people helping to get our food from farm to supermarket? Work can vary from operating heavy machinery to milking cows. A lot of this is very physical work, so you need to be fit – and the hours and demand for it vary throughout the year. So if you're looking for something for a short period, just to get you started, this could be for you.

2 _____ Especially in the early stages of large-scale projects, these guys get to spend a large percentage of their time outside on building sites, often braving the elements. They're easy to spot when sunbathing – they're the ones whose tans have developed around their high-viz vests.

3 _____ Although it's primarily an office-based role, in the right company you could be organising outside events. Entertaining clients is all part and parcel of the business world, so if you think you could handle regular corporate golf days or champagne lunches at a tennis match, then this is the job for you.

4 _____ And speaking of champagne lunches, you can't expect high-flying executives and VIP guests to pour their own drinks or collect their own food. The demand for waiting staff will always be high in the summer months (this is when you're likely to be rushed off your feet), so join an agency who can provide you with regular work throughout the year. It can also be a great opportunity to network with some potential employers.

5 _____ Snowboarding, horse riding, paintballing and countless other outdoor sports all require someone on hand to ensure everyone has a good time. What better way is there to make a living than doing something you love and making sure other people are happy?

6 _____ Potentially the healthiest group of workers in the UK, these people spend their days walking the streets of our town and city centres on the hunt for breaches of motoring laws. Unfortunately the uniform is not exactly ideal for scorching summer days. Also, you do unfortunately need to be prepared to deal with angry members of the public, and to keep your cool. No one likes to come back to their car to find they've been fined!

2 Which job does each paragraph describe?

Traffic wardens   Agricultural workers
Activity coordinators   Events managers
Construction workers   Catering staff

3 According to the paragraphs, which jobs:

a are usually temporary?

b require special clothing?

c involve working with customers or clients?

d require the worker to be physically active?

4 Which phrase tells you that

a farm workers do work that involves using their strength. p..................... w.....................

b construction workers have to work outside whatever the weather is like. b.....................
t..................... e.....................

c events managers spend a lot of time inside. o.....................-b..................... r.....................

d catering staff will be very busy r..................... o..................... y..................... f.....................

e activity coordinators earn money. m..................... a l.....................

f traffic wardens have to stay calm. k..................... y..................... c.....................

13a Qualifications in the UK

Type of activity
Reading; matching questions and answers. Individual or group work.

AECC reference
Rt/E3.4a; Rt/L1.5a

Aims
To develop learners' reading skills and knowledge of UK qualifications

Vocabulary
certificate, ESOL

Preparation
Photocopy one worksheet for each learner.

Differentiation
Stronger learners: do as a 'mingle' activity. You could photocopy the postings onto paper of one colour, and the responses onto different colours. Cut them up into strips of paper, then distribute one strip to each learner. Ask learners to mingle to find the match.

Weaker learners: Match the first two questions and responses together, and ask the learners to do the remaining two together.

Warmer
Depending on the age and level of qualifications of your learners, ask them what qualifications they have (either from the UK or their own country), or what they would like to have. Be sensitive about students who may not have taken any formal qualifications.

1 Give each learner a worksheet. Ask them to discuss the answers in pairs and then ask pairs to share their answers with the whole class.

2 Ask learners to read the postings alone, and then work with a partner to match the postings to the questions from task 1.

Answers
1 Include it or keep quiet?
2 Do I need to do another exam?
3 Can't find the course I want
4 A question of translation

3 Put learners in small groups to discuss these questions. Then ask learners to share their experiences with the whole class.

4 Explain that these are the responses to the postings. Ask learners to read them and then work with a partner to match them to the original postings by writing the correct name in the gap.

Answers
a Ela **b** Hussein **c** Vlad **d** Emeka

5 Ask learners to match the phrases and definitions.

Answers
Higher Education = The university system in the UK
Further Education = The college system in the UK
Vocational courses = Training connected to specific jobs
HNDs and HNCs = Qualifications to do specific jobs
IELTS = An English language exam which enables people to enter university
A levels = School exams that students in England, Wales and Northern Ireland take at the age of 18

Extension
Give each learner a role: half are college careers advisors, and the other half are students looking for information and/or advice about qualifications in the UK. You could allocate learners with the roles of the writers of the posts to the learners, or let them use their own ideas.

Links to other themes in this book
For more on qualifications, see 1a.

Answers: Self-study exercises

1 School: A levels, GCSEs **College:** A levels, GCSEs, degrees, HNDs
Universities: degrees, HNDS, PhDs

2 1 the 2 a 3 – 4 a 5 – 6 – 7 – 8 a
9 – 10 a 11 – 12 the 13 – 14 the 15 a

1 Look at the questions below which were posted on an internet site about UK qualifications. What do the four people want to know?

> Do I need to do another exam?   A question of translation
> Include it or keep quiet?   Can't find the course I want

2 Read the full text of the postings, and match them to the questions above.

1
I'm writing on behalf of my wife, whose English is elementary. She's passed some exams called ESOL Skills for Life at Entry 1. She's looking for work, and isn't sure whether to put these ESOL qualifications on her CV, because Entry 1 is the lowest level and people might think her English isn't very good. So perhaps it's better not to say anything at all about this. What do you think she should do?   Thanks, **Hussein, Stockport**

2
I did well at school in my country, and now I want to go to university in the UK. Will my school-leaving certificate (I did quite well in English) be enough to get me in? Or will the university test my English?   **Emeka, Zimbabwe**

3
I want to train as a plumber. They don't teach plumbing at my local uni. How can I find one that does?   **Vlad, Belfast**

4
I did the 'Matura' exam in Poland when I was 19. When I wrote that on an application form for a job, they asked me what it meant. So should I call it something different? Oh – it's the school-leaving exams, by the way!   **Ela, Cardiff, Wales**

3 Have you ever wanted to know the answers to any similar questions? What did you do to find out?

4 Read the responses below. Match them to the postings by writing the correct name in the gap.

a
Thank you, ………………………………………… – I didn't know that either. It sounds like the same sort of thing as A levels in the UK. So, should you describe them as A levels? Well, no, because if you haven't taken A levels, you can't say that you've got A levels. I think the best thing to do is use the name of the exam in your language in quotation marks, and add that it is 'equivalent to A levels'.

b
Any qualification is (a) worth having and (b) worth mentioning on your CV. If someone's English isn't great, the employer will soon find this out. But don't worry, …………………………………………, plenty of people have found work in the UK, even if their English isn't brilliant. And if someone mentions a recent qualification on their CV, this shows they are willing to learn. And employers like to see that.

d
…………………………………………, you're more likely to find one at your local college, as it's not a subject that's offered as a degree. Your local Further Education (FE) college will probably have a range of vocational courses, from a Higher National Diploma (HND) in Hospitality Management to a Higher National Certificate (HNC) in Hairdressing.

f
Your previous qualifications will help, …………………………………………, but institutions of Higher Education (HE) in the UK will expect you to have an internationally recognised English Language qualification if you're from a non-English-speaking country. The one that's widely used in the UK is called IELTS (International English Language Testing System). You should be able to find out more at your local college or university, or visit www.ielts.org. If you do well in this test, you can use it to help you get into any university in the UK, as well as many more overseas.

5 Match the words and phrases from the responses to the definitions.

Higher Education	An English language exam which enables people to enter university
Further Education	School exams that students in England, Wales and Northern Ireland take at the age of 18
Vocational courses	The college system in the UK
HNDs and HNCs	Training connected to specific jobs
IELTS	Qualifications to do specific jobs
A levels	The university system in the UK

13b Exam task practice

Type of activity
Discussing exam tips; practising reading and listening exam tasks. Individual work.

AECC reference
Rt/E3.4a; Lr/E3.2a; Rt/L1.5a; Lr/L1.2a

Aims
To develop learners' reading and listening skills in some of the task types common in ESOL for Work exams.

Vocabulary
reimburse, outstanding, risk assessment, fire drill

Preparation
Photocopy one worksheet for each learner. Check the answer to task 1c with the relevant exam board.

Differentiation
Stronger learners: give them the audioscript and ask them to identify any unknown vocabulary.

Weaker learners: pair them up with stronger learners after task 2 who can show them which the key phrases are.

Warmer
Find out how much the learners already know about the ESOL for Work exams. Discuss with them how they are different from other language exams they have taken.

Check the exam boards' websites for fuller details, remembering that there are substantial differences between the ESOL for Work exams offered by the different boards.

1 Give each learner a worksheet. Ask learners to discuss the tips in pairs. Note: make sure the learners are familiar with the exam regulations of whichever exam board you are using.

> **Answers**
> **a** F **b** T **c** (check with exam board)

2 Ask learners to work alone. Set a time limit of five minutes to answer the three questions.

> **Answers**
> **1** c **2** c **3** b

If any learners finish early, ask them to prepare an explanation as to why their chosen answer is correct, and why the other two answers are wrong. When conducting feedback, ask the early finishers to explain and justify their choices.

3 Ask learners to discuss the listening exam tips in pairs.

> **Answers**
> **a** T **b** T **c** F

4 (▶ 22 to 24) Ask the learners to read questions 1,2 and 3. Play the recordings. Conduct detailed feedback, discussing exactly why the answers are correct, replaying parts of the recording if necessary.

> **Answers**
> **1** a **2** b **3** b

5 Put learners in groups to discuss any other exam tips they know or have used in the past. Ask groups to share their ideas with the whole class. This should allow for any similarities and differences between exams that students have taken before in their own countries to be clarified. Point out that with multiple-choice questions, there is often one answer which they can discount altogether, and two others that it is harder to choose between. Explain to students that there are no minus points for getting an answer wrong.

Extension
If learners are taking English for Work or ESOL for Work exams, refer them to the websites of the exam board whose exam they are taking for fuller details and additional practice.

Answers: Self-study exercises

1 1 a 2 a 3 b 4 b 5 b

2 1 measure 2 exercising 3 quarter 4 settle
   5 outstanding

1 Look at the following pieces of advice about reading exams. Are they true (T) or false (F)?

a In a reading test, you need to understand every word of the text to be able to answer the question.

b It's important to give yourself enough time to answer all the questions.

c You can use a dictionary in the reading test.

2 Read the texts and choose the best answer.

1 Ali has written the note to
  a complain about the food.
  b apologise for a mistake.
  c warn staff.
	2 Mrs Lambert wants to
	  a place a new order.
	  b get a discount.
	  c have a refund.
		3 Mr Poznanski is
		  a making a payment.
		  b requesting a payment.
		  c acknowledging a payment.

Domenico's Sandwich Bar

Dear All,
I thought you should know - one of our customers called to say he'd found a hair in the takeaway sandwich he'd bought earlier. He was very angry, and he said he was going to come in and complain in person. If he does, please be apologetic.
Ali,
(Shift Manager)

Dear Sir or Madam,
ORDER NO. 86239845C
I understand that there is a 14-day cooling-off period on your services. As such, I wish to exercise my right to do so, as I have found the same level of cover at a substantially lower price elsewhere. I would be grateful if you could reimburse me for the full amount I have paid.
Yours faithfully,
Christine Lambert
Christine Lambert (Mrs)

Poznanski scaffolding limited

Dear Mr Smith,

Balance of £604.83

Further to our letter of June 8, your payment became due on June 16, and is still outstanding. However, should you have settled this balance in the meantime, please accept our thanks and disregard this letter.

We look forward to hearing from you.

A Poznanski

3 Look at the following pieces of advice about listening exams. Are they true (T) or false (F)?

a It's a good idea to read the question before listening to the recording.

b Don't expect to hear exactly the same words in the recording as you have in the question.

c You can ask for the recording to be played again if you did not hear the answer.

4 Read the three questions and then listen to the recordings.

Listening 1

A manager is describing his company's sales figures. Which graph is she describing?

a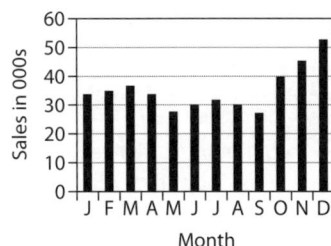

b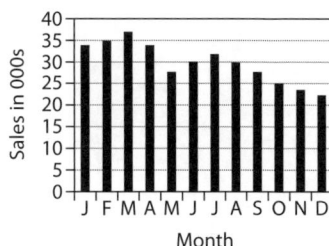

c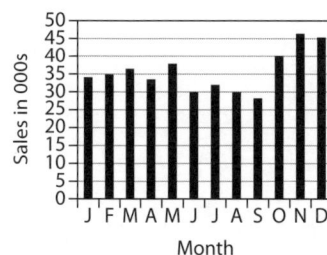

Listening 2

What is the man describing?

a risk assessment

b fire drill

c Health and Safety training

Listening 3

A woman is phoning a medical surgery. When is the woman going to visit the doctor?

a Tuesday

b Wednesday

c Thursday

13c Evaluating a student's exam performance

Type of activity
Reading, listening to and evaluating a learner's performance in writing and speaking exam practice tasks. Individual and pair work.

AECC reference
Lr/E3.1c; Lr/L1.6a; Sd/L1.1b; Wt/L1.3a

Aims
To develop learners' awareness of what constitutes effective performance in exams.

Vocabulary
inappropriate, apologetic, accurate, deliver, delivery, compensation, appropriate, impede, communication, aggressive

Preparation
Photocopy one worksheet for each learner.

Differentiation
Stronger learners: for task 6, have pairs of learners assess each other's performances.

Weaker learners: omit tasks 2 and 5 because the language may be too difficult.

Warmer
Ask if the learners can remember or guess what criteria writing exam answers are usually based on, and write suggestions on the board. Make sure you know the criteria that your exam board uses.

1 Give each learner a worksheet. Ask learners to read Fatima's answer and then discuss with a partner how well they think she did. Ask learners to share their comments with the whole class.

2 Ask learners to look at the examiner feedback, and decide which comment is more appropriate.

> **Answers**
> answered the question fully; is suitably apologetic; too long; consistently accurate

3 Ask the learners to do this task alone; remind them to try and meet the criteria as they write.

4 Ask learners to read the rubric for the speaking exam practice, and choose the correct answer.

> **Answers**
> c

5 (▶23) Explain that you are going to play an extract from a mock ESOL for Work Speaking exam. Ask learners to evaluate the candidate's performance. Play the recording.

> **Answers**
> was appropriate and sensible; but it does not impede communication; firmly but politely; mostly accurate
>
> Fatima makes just 3 minor errors (which you could ask learners if they noticed): *According our contract, would you able, do something with price*

6 Ask learners to perform the same role play in pairs, taking it in turns to be the examiner and the candidate. Discuss as a class how learners felt they performed.

Extension
For additional ESOL for Work Speaking and Writing exam practice, you could access (or refer the learners to) your exam board's website.

Answers: Self-study exercises

1 1 ~~negotiationer~~ negotiator   2 ~~deliverment~~ delivery
   3 ✓   4 ~~unappropriate~~ inappropriate   5 ✓
2 1 c   2 d   3 b   4 a

1 Look at the writing task and the candidate's answer.

You had a problem getting to work this morning and arrived late. Write an email to your line manager about this, explaining: • when you arrived • what the problem was • what you propose to do about it. Write 50–60 words.	Dear Malcolm, I just wanted to write you a quick email to let you know that I was held up in traffic on my way to work this morning, so unfortunately I arrived 30 minutes late, at 9.30. Luckily the shop was not too busy, but if you like, I can stay an extra 30 minutes one evening to make up for the lost time. With apologies for any inconvenience, Fatima

2 Look at the assessor's comments, and circle the more appropriate underlined option.

Name : Fatima Ismail

ANSWER   The candidate has _answered the question fully / only addressed two out of three content points_.

REGISTER   The email _adopts an inappropriate tone / is suitably apologetic_.

LENGTH   The answer is _too long / the right length_.

ACCURACY   The language is _consistently accurate / mostly accurate_.

3 Now write your own answer to the question.

4 Read the candidate's instruction booklet from the speaking test. What is going to happen in this part of the test?

a The examiner is going to interview the candidate.
b The candidate is going to give a presentation.
c The examiner and candidate are going to perform a role play together.

Candidate task

You have one minute to read through this task.

Information exchange

Your company has ordered and paid a 50% deposit for some computer equipment. The examiner works for the company that delivers the equipment, but it has not been delivered yet. You are telephoning him/her to discuss the situation.

Find out:

1 why the equipment has not been delivered

2 when the delivery will take place

3 if the company can provide any compensation for the delay.

You will then be asked if you are satisfied with the outcome of the discussion.

---

5 Now listen to Fatima doing the speaking exam. Look at the examiner's comments about her performance in the exam and circle the more appropriate underlined option.

Fatima clarified what to do at the start of the activity, which _suggests that she is a weak candidate / was appropriate and sensible_.

She has a pronounced accent, _but it does not impede communication / which makes her difficult to understand_.

She made her complaint _firmly but politely / in an aggressive manner_.

The language is _consistently accurate / mostly accurate_.

---

6 Now work in pairs and perform the role play together. How well did you do?

14a Telephoning

Type of activity
Listening to telephone conversations. Pair work.

AECC reference
Sd/E3.1f; Sd/E3.1b; Sd/L1.2c; Sd/L1.1b

Aims
To develop learners' ability to talk effectively and politely on the phone.

Vocabulary
fully booked, give sb a ring, get through, deliver, switchboard, time slot

Preparation
Photocopy one worksheet for each learner. For task 4, make one extra copy for every two learners and cut the worksheet up as indicated.

Differentiation
Stronger learners: before listening to track 27 again in task 5, ask them to try and remember the missing parts of the conversation.

Weaker learners: play track 27 right through before doing task 4.

Warmer
Ask the learners when they last spoke on the phone in English, whether they sometimes have any problems speaking on the phone in English, and how they deal with these.

1 Give each learner the top half of the worksheet. Ask the learners to work in pairs to predict what the speakers say. Suggest that they pencil in possible answers (each gap has one or two words).

2 (▶26) Ask learners to listen and check as you play the recording. Ask learners to practice the conversation with a partner. In feedback, ask questions to reinforce their understanding of the phrases commonly used in phone conversations. Ask questions such as:

Would speaker B say 'I am Mrs Brady speaking'? (No.)

Why does speaker A say '<u>I'm afraid</u> we're fully booked'? (The speaker says 'I'm afraid' to introduce bad news.)

Answers
1 through to 2 speaking 3 this is
4 mind holding 5 I'm afraid 6 sound
7 Thanks for 8 Cheerio

3 Give half the learners Alice's half of the conversation (A), and give the other learners Huda's half (B). Give them 30 seconds to read through their half of the conversation and answer these questions:

What is the conversation about? (rearranging a delivery)

Do the speakers know each other? (probably not)

Put learners in small groups with learners who have the same half of the conversation. Ask them to work out what the second person in the dialogue says, and to write this in pencil in the gap. Explain that the purpose is not to guess the 'correct' answer, but to think of a suitably polite response. Monitor closely.

4 Pair up the learners so that each learner A sits with a learner B. Ask them to compare answers. Ask learners if they noticed any natural-sounding phrases in the conversation which they think could be useful for them to use in future telephone conversations. Possible suggestions:

• *There's a bit of a problem.*

• *I thought I'd give you a ring.*

• *It took ages to get through.*

5 (▶27) Play the recording while learners listen and check. Play the recording a second time for consolidation.

Answers
See audioscript (track 27, p. 128).

Extension
Ask learners to produce a similar gapped phone conversation exercise for their classmates to complete. This could be an imagined phone conversation between an employee at the learner's place of work and a member of the public. Monitor, and encourage learners to word their contributions politely. Encourage them to use softening devices like 'a bit', 'I'm afraid', etc. in order to make the conversation sound natural.

Links to other themes in this book
For more on phoning, see 7c and 10a.

Answers: Self-study exercises

1 1 a 2 a 3 b 4 a

2 through to; that; This; speaking; line; Sure; sound; what name was it; help

1 Read the telephone conversation between a hairdresser and a customer. Can you guess what the missing words and phrases are?

A: Good morning, you're (1)....................
.... Harrow Haircuts.
B: Oh hello, is that Ana (2)....................?
A: This is Ana, yes. How can I help?
B: Hello Ana, (3)......................................
Mrs Brady speaking.
A: Morning Mrs Brady, how are you today?
B: Not bad, thanks, yes. Errm, any chance of an appointment this afternoon?
A: I'll just get the diary. Would you (4)...............................?

B: Not at all, that's fine.
A: (5)........................... we're fully booked this afternoon. But would tomorrow afternoon be OK?
B: What time?
A: How does 3.30 (6)...................?
B: Oh, that's fine, yes, 3.30.
A: OK, well, look forward to seeing you tomorrow, then. (7)........................... calling.
B: Right, OK, then. (8)...................!

2 Listen and check.

Conversations for tasks 3–5

A: Alice
Huda works for Niceprice Online Supermarket, and answers calls from customers who want to discuss their orders. He receives a call from a customer called Alice. Try to complete her side of the conversation.

Huda: ....
Alice: Oh hello, my name's Alice.
Huda: ....
Alice: Yes, it's ACC512.
Huda: ....
Alice: Well, there's a bit of a problem with my order.
Huda: ....
Alice: No, it's not that. I booked the delivery for tomorrow. But I have to go out.
Huda: ....
Alice: Yes, that's right. I wasn't sure if I could do it on the Internet, so I thought I'd give you a ring.
Huda: ....
Alice: OK, well, perhaps I'll do that next time. It took ages to get through – I've been on hold for hours.
Huda: ....
Alice: Can we arrange it for Thursday about 4 o'clock?
Huda: ....
Alice: OK, well, that's fine then.
Huda: ....
Alice: No, that's fine, thank you very much for your help.
Huda: ....

B: Huda
Alice does her food shopping online with Niceprice Supermarkets, who deliver her shopping to her home. She calls Niceprice, and speaks to Huda. Try to complete her side of the conversation.

Huda: Niceprice Online Supermarkets. You're through to Huda. Can I take your name, please?
Alice: ....
Huda: Morning Alice. Could I have your customer reference number please?
Alice: ....
Huda: OK then, Alice. So how can I help you today?
Alice: ....
Huda: Right, so do you mean the wrong things were delivered?
Alice: ....
Huda: I see. So you need to change the delivery time then?
Alice: ....
Huda: Oh, well, you can, actually. It's quite easy to do online, just go to 'my account' and then click on 'change delivery details'. Just so you know for future reference.
Alice: ....
Huda: Yes, I'm afraid the switchboard has been very busy today. Anyway, when would you like to rearrange the delivery for?
Alice: ....
Huda: Well, we can't guarantee the time, but we can give you a time slot of between 2 and 5 in the afternoon.
Alice: ....
Huda: Was there anything else I can help you with today?
Alice: ....
Huda: Well, you've been talking to Huda. Thank you very much for your call to Niceprice.

14b Service with a smile

Type of activity
Listening to service encounters. Individual and pair work.

AECC reference
Sc/E3.1a; Sc/E3.3; Sc/L1.1a; Lr/L1.2b

Aims
To raise learners' awareness of what sounds polite.

Vocabulary
Hawaiian, roughly, give someone a shout, tenner, shut, till

Preparation
Photocopy one worksheet for each learner.

Differentiation
Stronger learners: let stronger learners work independently, checking their answers against the audioscript at an earlier stage.

Weaker learners: give a copy of the audioscript to learners who have difficulty transcribing.

Warmer
Ask learners how important being polite is considered in Britain. (Likely answer: very).

1 Give each learner a worksheet. Discuss the sign 'The customer is always right' as a whole group.

2 Ask learners to read the skeleton dialogues quickly to find the answers to the question.

> **Answers**
> Thabo works in a takeaway; Adam works on a bus.

3 (▶28) Explain to learners that they are going to hear two versions of Thabo's conversation. Explain that you will play version A first for students to read and listen to. Play the recording and then discuss the questions as a whole class. You may wish to play the recording again, pausing after Thabo's turns.

> **Answers**
> Thabo is not very polite.
> **1** No greeting; he sounds annoyed.
> **2** A one-word answer often sounds rude, especially if it is 'What?'
> **3** He sounds irritated that the customer is not spending more money.
> **4** He is telling the customer what to do, rather than politely asking him to sit and wait.
> **5** He sounds annoyed with the customer's question.

4 (▶29) Play the recording and discuss the question as a whole class.

> **Answers**
> This version is a big improvement: all the problems above are resolved. Thabo now sounds friendly and polite, and seems happy to serve the customer.

5 (▶29) Play the recording again, and ask learners to write what they hear on line b for each utterance.

> **Answers**
> See audioscript (track 29, p. 128).

6 (▶30–31) Repeat steps 3–5 for Adam's conversations.

> **Answers**
> See audioscript (tracks 30–31, p. 128) for text.
> **1** The one-word answer sounds unfriendly.
> **2** This is OK but sounds a little abrupt.
> **3** He simply repeats what he said before, but louder, which is unlikely to help if the passenger did not understand.
> **4** Again, a one-word answer sounds unfriendly.
> **5** He seems to be criticizing the passenger here.
> **6** He tells the customer what to do, which again sounds rude.

7 Put learners in pairs or groups, and ask them to write the checklist.

> **Suggested answers**
> DO... smile; say 'please' and 'thank you'; use friendly intonation
>
> DON'T... sound annoyed; give one-word answers; criticize the customer; tell the customer what to do; speak in a monotone; raise your voice

8 Ask learners to work in pairs to read and improve the third dialogue, making it more polite. (For the non-Welsh speakers: Ar gau is Welsh for closed.)

9 (▶32) Play the recording. Allow learners to compare their version with the recorded one.

Extension
Ask learners to write a dialogue between a member of staff and a customer in one of the workplaces from task 2.

Links to other themes in this book
For more on improving dialogues, see 3b and 4a.

> ### Answers: Self-study exercises
>
> **1** 1 a   2 c   3 a   4 a

1 Look at the sign. Is this always true?

2 Read the two conversations below. Where do Thabo, and Adam work? Choose from the following.

> Remember – the customer is always right

| on a bus | in a surgery reception | in a takeaway | in a supermarket |

Conversation 1

Thabo: (1) A What do you want?

  B ....

Customer: Erm, can I get one Hawaiian, please?

Thabo: (2) A What?

  B ....

Customer: Could I have one Hawaiian, please?

Thabo: (3) A Is that all you're going to buy?

  B ....

Customer: Just the pizza, please.

Thabo: (4) A Sit down and wait.

  B ....

Customer: OK, do you know roughly how long it'll be?

Thabo: (5) A Look, I'll do it as quick as I can. Alright?

  B ....

Customer: OK, fine, I'll sit here and wait.

Conversation 2

Customer: Oh hello, does this go to Station Road?

Adam: (1) A Yes.

  B ....

Customer: Oh good. One then, please.

Adam: (2) A Single or return?

  B ....

Customer: Sorry?

Adam: (3) A Single or return?

  B ....

Customer: Oh, I see, well, yes. Just a single then.

Adam: (4) A A pound.

  B ....

Customer: Right, here's a tenner.

Adam: (5) A I don't want that. I want a pound.

  B ....

Customer: Oh, let's see what I've got. Oh yes, here you are.

Adam: (6) A Take your ticket.

  B ....

3 Read and listen to conversation 1: version A. How polite was Thabo? Can you make his answers more polite?

4 Listen to version B of the conversation. Is this better? Why?

5 Listen again and write what Thabo says now.

6 Repeat steps 3–5 for Adam.

7 Write a checklist for how to sound more polite when talking with customers:

DO ☑ ....

  ☑ ....

  ☑ ....

DON'T ☒ ....

  ☒ ....

  ☒ ....

> CLOSED
> AR GAU

8 Read the dialogue below, and make it more polite.

Customer: You're not closing yet, are you?

Shop assistant: Can't you see the time? It's 8:30 – that means we're closed!

Customer: Oh, please, I just want a bottle of milk.

Shop assistant: I don't care what you want, I said we're CLOSED!

Customer: But I'm a regular customer. I come here every day.

Shop assistant: Look, I don't care who you are. WE ARE CLOSED!

9 Listen to an improved version and compare it with your version.

14c Customer service Snakes and Ladders

Type of activity
Role playing service encounters; playing a board game.
Group work.

AECC reference
Sd/E3.1b; Sc/E3.4d; Sc/L1.1b

Aims
To provide learners with practice at polite interaction with members of the public in a work context.

Vocabulary
appointment, unavailable, till, bill, elderly

Preparation
Photocopy one worksheet for each group of three or four learners. You will need one dice for each group, and different counters for moving around the board.

Differentiation
Stronger learners: group stronger learners together so that they can fully develop the conversations.

Weaker learners: ask other learners to read the scenarios for learners who have problems reading.

For a larger board, enlarge onto A3 paper.

Warmer

Ask the learners if they played Snakes and Ladders, or any other board game, as children. Show the board and explain the basic principle of Snakes and Ladders (i.e. when you land on a ladder, you go up; when you land on a snake you go down). Explain that they are going to play this game while practising speaking politely to customers.

1 Put learners in groups of three or four. Give each group a worksheet (the Snakes and Ladders board), a dice and a counter each. Ask learners to put their counter on the START square.

2 Demonstrate how the game works with one of the groups:

- The first player rolls the dice and moves forward that number of squares.

- If a player lands at the bottom of a ladder, they move to the square at the top of the ladder. The next player then takes their turn.

- If a player lands at the head of a snake, they move to the square at the bottom of the snake. The next player then takes their turn.

- If a player lands at the top of a ladder, or at the bottom of a snake, nothing happens. The next player then takes their turn.

- If a player lands on a square with a scenario, the player must role play the situation, taking care to be suitably polite. As the role plays involve two people, the turn-taker must choose one of the other players to take part in the role play. For example, a player landing on square 3 plays the part of the newsagent and another learner in the group would play the part of the customer.

- After each role play, the other players in the group comment on how effectively they feel the roles were played.

- When the role play is finished, the player stays on the square. It is then the turn of the next player.

- The winner is the player who reaches the FINISH square first.

Suggested answers

2 Excuse me, are you thinking of buying that? It's just that, you know, we need to keep all the magazines in a saleable condition … .

4 Oh hello, look, I'm afraid we've had to give your appointment to someone else as you weren't here on time. But would you like to make another appointment? I'll just get the diary …

6 Good morning, would you like any help at all?

8 I'm afraid the manager isn't actually available at the moment, but is there any way I can help?

10 I'm afraid we've just closed, actually. Sorry, the till's already off. But we're open again at 9.30 tomorrow if you're able to come back then.

12 I'm sorry. You've only given me £40, and it's £45.99, so do you have another £5.99?

14 I'm afraid we don't open for another 15 minutes, so would you be able to come back then?

16 Sorry, could I just ask you to keep your voice down if you want to use your phone?

18 Excuse me, it's actually no smoking here, so could I ask you to either put it out, or go outside.

20 Can I take your name, please?

22 I'm terribly sorry, but I'm afraid there's been a problem, and we're going to have to cancel your booking for tomorrow.

24 I'm sorry. I'll bring you a fresh plate immediately.

26 I do apologise, I'll go and chase it up for you.

28 Would you like a hand with the bags? Shall I pop them in the boot for you?

Extension

Ask the learners to act out one or more of the dialogues in front of the class, with other students commenting on how polite they feel the speakers were.

Links to other themes in this book
For more on customer service, see 12a.

Answers: Self-study exercises

1 1 b 2 b 3 c 4 c 5 a 6 a
2 1 b 2 b 3 a

Customer service Snakes and Ladders (14c)

30 FINISH	**29**	**28** You are a taxi driver. An elderly passenger is getting in with heavy bags. Offer to help them.	**27**	**26** You work in a café. A customer is complaining that she has been waiting 30 minutes for her lunch.
21	**22** You work in a beauty therapist's. You need to phone a customer who has an appointment tomorrow and cancel their booking.	**23**	**24** You work in a restaurant. A customer is complaining that you have brought them cold chips.	**25**
20 You work for a taxi firm. A customer calls to order a taxi. Find out: the customer's name, phone number, address, destination. Tell them what time the car will arrive.	**19**	**18** A customer has lit a cigarette in a non-smoking area. Explain this to them.	**17**	**16** You work in a bookshop. A customer is speaking very loudly on his mobile phone, Other customers are complaining.
11	**12** A customer is paying a bill in cash. The bill is for £45.99, but they have only given you £40.	**13**	**14** A customer wants to come into the shop where you work, but you do not open for another 15 minutes.	**15**
10 A customer wants to buy something, but you have just closed the till.	**9**	**8** A customer wants to see the manager. Explain that the manager is unavailable, and ask if you can help instead.	**7**	**6** You work in a clothes shop. A customer seems to be looking for something in the shop. Ask if you can help them.
1 START	**2** You work in a newsagent's. A lady comes in every day, and reads magazines for half an hour, then leaves without buying anything. Explain to her that this is not allowed.	**3**	**4** You work in a hairdresser's. Mr Smith has arrived 15 minutes late for his appointment and the hairdresser is no longer available. Explain that the next available appointment is tomorrow.	**5**

15a Email or snail mail?

Type of activity
Sorting vocabulary items. Individual and pair work.

AECC reference
Rw/E3.3a; Rw/L1.1a; Wt/L1.4a

Aims
To develop learners' vocabulary related to email; raise awareness of cultural sensitivities regarding the sending of work emails

Vocabulary
colleague, invoice, resignation, contract, correspondence, value

Preparation
Photocopy one worksheet for each learner and provide monolingual dictionaries.

Differentiation
IT literacy: you could group any learners who are not IT literate / computer users with those who are, and encourage peer teaching.

Warmer
You could draw a snail on the board, and ask what connotations it has for the learners. Ask what they think 'snail mail' means, and why the term is used. Ask learners whether they use email or 'snail mail' more frequently, and for what kind of things. Find out from the learners how often they use email at work or for personal reasons, and what they like and dislike about using email.

1 Give each learner a worksheet. Ask learners to discuss the options in pairs, and then discuss as a whole class.

> **Answers**
> **a** email
> **b** phone
> **c** snail mail (or email)
> **d** probably snail mail, though perhaps an e-card
> **e** probably a letter by snail mail or internal mail
> **f** snail mail

2 Ask learners to work alone to sort the vocabulary and then ask them to check answers in small groups. They may wish to use dictionaries. Explain that they may use some words twice.

> **Answers**
> **a** collection time; parcel; frank; stamp; postbox; enclose; draft
> **b** letterbox; parcel; delivery; collection time
> **c** sent folder; attachment; outbox; upload; attach
> **d** inbox; attachment; delivery; download

3 Ask learners to look quickly at Texts A and B and elicit what kind of text they are (a notice and an email). Ask learners to work alone to choose the correct words (1–8) and then check answers in small groups.

> **Answers**
> **1** postbox
> **2** franking
> **3** parcel
> **4** enclosing
> **5** a draft
> **6** inbox
> **7** download
> **8** attach

Extension
Ask learners to write another two pieces of advice for sending emails. You could also direct learners to this website: http://jerz.setonhill.edu/writing/etext/e-mail.htm, which has ten tips for writing emails.

Links to other themes in this book
For more on emails, see 10b and 16a.

Answers: Self-study exercises

1 1 d 2 b 3 c 4 a 5 f 6 h 7 e 8 g

2 1 upload 2 enclose 3 attach 4 snail mail
  5 inbox 6 proof of postage 7 draft
  8 postbox

1 What form of communication would you use in the following situations (email, 'snail mail' or other)?

a You want to contact a colleague to arrange a meeting with her next week.
b You urgently need to speak to a colleague before the end of the day.
c You need to send an invoice to a customer.
d A colleague has just had a baby and you want to send her a card.
e You are sending your resignation to your boss.
f A customer has emailed you a contract, which they have asked you to sign and return.

2 Look at the words in the box. Do you associate the words in the box with 'snail mail' or email? And with sending or receiving? Put them in the right place in the grid.

sent folder   letterbox   attach   parcel   delivery   collection time   inbox
upload   draft   stamp   frank   attachment   postbox   enclose   outbox   download

	sending	receiving
snail	a	b
@	c	d

3 Plantsdirect is an online store selling gardening equipment. Read texts A and B and complete them by choosing the correct word.

A

Notice to all employees

Several items of value have disappeared in the post on the way to our customers. We have therefore decided to revise our external post procedures.

Please do not send any correspondence from a public **(1)** _letterbox / postbox_, as we need to retain proof of postage. Instead, please arrange for our Administration Department to arrange the postage of all items as detailed below.

We have now purchased a **(2)** _franking / stamp_ machine. This is a device for sending mail which calculates the cost of sending the letter or **(3)** _parcel / attachment_ based on size and weight, and prints the price of postage. However, if you are **(4)** _enclosing / attaching_ any items of value, or if you have any queries, please contact Sally on Extension 2396, or email at admin@plantsdirect.co.uk.

B

From: JorgKopps@Plantsdirect.co.uk
Subject: a query

Hello Sally,

Thank you for the information about franking. I guess that means no more trips to the post office, which should save lots of time!

I've got another enquiry for you. It's about email. A customer has lost the receipt we sent him, and has asked for a replacement. I know this is probably standard procedure, but I haven't done this before, so I wonder if I could send you **(5)** _a draft / an outbox_ of my mail to him BEFORE I send the real thing? That way, you could tell me if I've done it right.

And how do I know that when I email him, the mail will go to his **(6)** _inbox / outbox_ and not into a junk-mail folder? Is there anything I can do? Also, he said on the phone that his computer won't let him **(7)** _frank / download_ PDF files, so can I just **(8)** _enclose / attach_ a Word document and send him that?

Sorry if these seem like really obvious questions, but as you know, I only started last week, so I've still got a lot to learn!

Many thanks in advance for your help,

Jorg

15b Getting it right

Type of activity
Multiple-choice quiz; correcting a letter. Individual, pair and group work.

AECC reference
Sc/E3.4a; Sc/L1.3a; Ws/L1.3a

Aims
To provide accuracy practice.

Preparation
Make and cut up enough copies of Student A's and Student B's portions of the worksheet for each learner to have one copy. Additionally, photocopy one worksheet for each learner as a written record.

Differentiation
Stronger learners: ask them to invent their own quiz, using quizzes A and B as models.

Weaker learners: give them the answers and put them in the role of the teacher, checking other learners' answers.

Warmer
If possible, put the learners into first-language groups (i.e. one group of Arabic speakers, one group of French speakers, etc.), though this is not essential. Ask the learners what differences there are between their own language and English as regards saying and writing addresses, dates, numbers, etc. Ask each group to feed back to the whole class. Ask if they know of any differences between the American and British systems of writing dates.

1 Give half the class quiz A, and the other half quiz B. Put learners in pairs with another learner who has the same quiz as them. Ask each pair to work together to answer the quiz questions. Monitor each pair's answers individually.

> **Answers**
> QUIZ A: **1** b **2** c **3** b **4** a **5** b **6** a **7** b
> QUIZ B: **1** a **2** c **3** b **4** a **5** b **6** c **7** c

2 Now pair up learners who did quiz A with learners who did quiz B, and ask them to try out their quiz on their new partner.

3 Ask learners to stay in pairs. Ask them them to read the letter, and to find and correct the errors.

> **Answers**
> Here are eight mistakes:
> CR Catering
> ~~Howards Lane 176~~ 176 Howards Lane
> ~~S21 6MW~~
> SHEFFIELD
> S21 6MW
> ~~29 April Thursday~~ [no year?]
> Thursday 29 April

> Dear Sir or Madam,
> This is to acknowledge receipt of your payment of ~~521.00£~~, [£521.00], which was received on ~~4/27~~. [April 27 / 27 April.] Please be advised that the sum of ~~£12,62.00~~ [£1,262] is also now due, with a deadline for payment of ~~May the 27th~~ [27 May]. Please note that this includes the discount of £42.50.
> Thank you for your continuing custom.
> Carol Roston
> Manager

Extension
Discussion: Ask learners if they have ever had difficulty saying or understanding any of the following in English: prices, web, email or postal addresses, numbers or dates. Ask them what happened, and what caused the misunderstanding. Reassure them by pointing out that it is not uncommon for native speakers to have similar misunderstandings.

Links to other themes in this book
For more on numeracy, see 9b, 15c and 16c.

> **Answers: Self-study exercises**
> **1** 1 ~~five bucks~~ 2 ~~nine nine nine~~ 3 ~~two pounds~~
> 4 ~~oh one double six nine triple eight double four~~
> 5 ~~3/1~~

1 Work with a partner and choose the best answer.

QUIZ A

PRICES

1 How is 'five pounds' written?
   a 5£   b £5   c 5£

2 'Ten grand' is slang for …
   a 10 p   b £10   c £10,000

NUMBERS

3 How do you say the number 2,172?
   a two thousand, one hundred seventy two
   b two thousand, one hundred and seventy two
   c two thousand, and one hundred and seventy two

DATES

4 Which is *not* considered a correct way to say the date April 30?
   a April thirty
   b the thirtieth of April
   c April the thirtieth

ADDRESSES

5 Which is the correct way to write an address?
   a 43 West road
   b 43 West Road
   c West Road 43

6 What is the last thing you write in an address?
   a The postcode
   b The town/city
   c The street

INTERNET/EMAIL

7 How would you say the address www.bbc.co.uk/news?
   a Triple W dot B B C dot co dot U K forward slash news
   b W W W dot B B C dot co dot U K forward slash news
   c Triple W full stop B B C full stop co full stop U K dash news

2 Now find a new partner who has not done Quiz A. Ask them the questions.

1 Work with a partner and choose the best answer.

QUIZ B

PRICES

1 Which of the following groups of words all mean 'pounds'?
   a quid, sterling   b bucks, quid   c sterling, bucks

2 Which is *not* a correct way to say £27.82?
   a Twenty seven eighty two
   b Twenty seven pounds eighty two
   c Twenty seven point eight two pounds

NUMBERS

3 What is the usual way to write the number one million?
   a 1000000   b 1,000,000   c 1.000.000

DATES

4 In British English and American English, what does the date 9/4 mean?
   a April 9 in the UK; September 4 in the USA
   b April 9 in the US; September 4 in the UK
   c September 4 in the UK and the USA

ADDRESSES

5 Which is the usual way to write a postcode?
   a BS 66 TK   b BS6 6TK   c BS66TK

6 Which word is often written in capital letters on an address, especially on an envelope?
   a The name of the company (JONES ELECTRONICS, Green Mews, Leeds, LS1 5AY)
   b The name of the road (Jones Electronics, GREEN MEWS, Leeds, LS1 5AY)
   c The name of the town (Jones Electronics, Green Mews, LEEDS, LS1 5AY)

INTERNET/EMAIL

7 How would you say the email address tom_jones@hassop.ac.uk?
   a Tom hyphen Jones at Hassop dot A C dot UK
   b Tom dash Jones at Hassop full stop A C full stop UK
   c Tom underscore Jones at Hassop dot A C dot UK

2 Now find a new partner who has not done Quiz B. Ask them the questions.

3 Look at the letter. How many mistakes can you find? Correct the mistakes.

CR Catering
Howards Lane 176
S21 6MW
SHEFFIELD

29 April Thursday

Dear Sir or Madam,

This is to acknowledge receipt of your payment of 521.00£, which was received on 4/27. Please be advised that the sum of £12,62.00 is also now due, with a deadline for payment of the 27th May. Please note that this includes the discount of £42.5.

Thank you for your continuing custom.

Carol Roston

Manager

(15c) Checking details

Type of activity
Information checking activity for groups of four learners. Group work.

AECC reference
Sd/E3.1f; Sd/E3.2b; Sd/L1.4a

Aims
To give learners practice at clarifying arrangements including times, addresses, prices, costs and email addresses

Vocabulary
venue, hang on, double-check, mix-up, inaccurate

Preparation
Photocopy one worksheet per learner, and cut them up to make enough for each learner to have the top section of the sheet, as well as a small Student 1, 2, 3 or 4 role card.

Differentiation
Stronger learners: set them the additional challenge of trying to use every one of the phrases from task 3.

Weaker learners: highlight the key information on their rolecards for task 4.

Warmer
Ask the learners if they have ever made arrangements which went wrong, e.g. one of the people got the wrong day, time or venue. Find out what happened, and what caused the problem.

1 (▶33) Give each learner a worksheet. Explain that a group of people are travelling to the same training day and are checking the arrangements. Some of the details are wrong. Play the recording and ask learners to say what the correct information is.

> **Answers**
> The training is in the month of November, not October.

2 Explain that the learners are going to study some language which is useful for clarifying, interrupting and correcting politely. Ask them to look at sentences a–k, and ask which ones they remember hearing. Play the recording again, and ask learners to tick the ones they hear.

> **Answers**
> a; b; d; f; h and i. Note: all the other expressions are correct, and would also be appropriate.

3 Explain that the learners are now going to conduct a similar discussion. Put learners in groups of three or four, and give each learner in each group a different role card. Ask learners to work alone to find the answers to the questions and make sure they don't show their cards to the others in their group. It is not necessary to conduct feedback at this stage.

4 Ask learners to work together to check the information they have about the training day. Tell learners that most of the information on their role card is correct, but there are two mistakes. Explain that where there is a difference, the one learner with different information (e.g. a different date, time or phone number) has the wrong information and needs to correct it.

> **Answers**
> **Student 1**   1: Address is 14 Sydney Grove, not 40
>
>   2: train arrives at 9.32, not 9.13
>
> **Student 2**   1: book before 27/7 not 27/6 for a £45 fee
>
>   2: postcode is 4US, not 4UF
>
> **Student 3**   1: Doreen Carmet's tel no begins 07948, not 07978
>
>   2: the ticket is £37.50 single, not return
>
> **Student 4**   1: training is till 4.30 pm, not 5.30 pm
>
>   2: organized by HEG events, not Doreen Carmet events

Extension
Learners could be sent on a real-world fact-finding mission, where each learner finds out about a coming event in their town (e.g. a concert, fireworks display, carnival), collecting details of the time, date, location, web address for further details, etc. Learners then dictate these details to each other.

Links to other themes in this book
For more on numeracy, see 9b and 16c.

Answers: Self-study exercises

1 ~~checking~~ to check; ~~mix-out~~ mix-up; ~~unaccurate~~ inaccurate; ~~double-verify~~ double-check; ~~disunderstanding~~ misunderstanding

1 Listen to four colleagues checking the information about a training day they are going to. One of them has one of the details wrong. What is the correct information?

2 Listen again. Which of these phrases did you hear? Put a tick (✓).

a We just need to check …

b Hang on, are you sure …?

c Sorry, what was that again?

d OK, so there's a mix-up here.

e Would you mind just repeating that, please?

f I'll just cross that out.

g Sorry, my information was inaccurate.

h Can I just double-check that?

i Is that definitely right?

j I don't think that's quite right.

k Really? It says here …

3 Your teacher will give you a role card. You are going to attend a training day with some colleagues and you need to check the details. Underline the information that gives you the answers to these questions, but do not show your card to anyone.

   a When and where is the training day?
   b What details do you have about the venue?
   c Who is the training organized by? What contact details do you have?
   d How can you travel to the venue, and how much will it cost?

4 Work in groups. Check the information you have about the training day, and correct any of the details on your card if necessary. Use some of the phrases from task 2.

Rolecards for tasks 3–4

Student 1

Training organized by HEG Events (tel. 0117 876 8392)

Contact person at HEG: Doreen Carmet (07948 927 395; Doreen_carmet@hegevents.co.uk)

Event venue: North Hotel, 40 Sydney Grove, Newcastle, NE3 4US

Training: 22/11. 10am–4.30pm

Cost: £55 (£45 if booked before 27 July)

Train to Newcastle. Dep. 0715; Arr. 0913 (£37.50 single)

Student 2

Training (22/11. 10am–4.30pm)

7.15 am train to Newcastle. Gets in 9.32 (£37.50 single)

at North Hotel, 14 Sydney Grove, Newcastle, NE3 4UF

Organizers: HEG Events (tel. 0117 876 8392)

Contact person at HEG: Doreen Carmet (07948 927 395; Doreen.carmet@hegevents.co.uk)

Costs £55 to attend (£45 if booked before 27/6)

Student 3

Training (Nov 22. 10am–4.30pm) organized by HEG Events (tel. 0117 876 8392 / Doreen Carmet on 07978 927 395) Doreen.carmet@hegevents.co.uk)

Event venue: North Hotel, 14 Sydney Grove, Newcastle, NE3 4US

Training costs £45 early booking fee (but this goes up to £55 after 27 July)

Train >Newcastle. leaves 0715; Arrives 0932 (£37.50 return)

Student 4

Training organized by Doreen Carmet Events Limited

Doreen Carmet: 07948 927 395; Doreen.carmet@hegevents.co.uk

Training at North Hotel, 14 Sydney Grove, Newcastle, NE3 4US

Date: 22 November

Time: 10 – 5.30

Training costs £45 before 27 July; £55 thereafter

Train >Newcastle. leaves 7.15 am; Arrives 9.32 (£37.50 single)

16a Moving on

Type of activity
Comparing different emails connected with leaving a job. Individual and group work.

AECC reference
Rt/E3.1a; Wt/E3.2a; Rt/L1.1a; Wt/L1.3a

Aims
To develop learners' awareness of appropriate register and develop writing skills.

Vocabulary
exit interview, Inland Revenue, reference, resignation letter

Preparation
Photocopy one worksheet for each learner and cut it in half.

Photocopy and cut up the bottom half of the worksheet so that you have one set of nine cards for each three or four learners.

Differentiation
Kinesthetic learners: give one slip of paper to each learner. Ask learners to mingle and organise themselves into groups for each email and to stand in the right sequence.

Weaker learners: give out the slips of paper for just one or two of the emails.

Warmer
Ask learners when they last left a job, who they told they were leaving, and what they did on their last day.

1 Give each learner the top half of the worksheet. Put learners into small groups of three or four and ask them to discuss the questions.

> **Answers**
> **a** If you work for a larger company, you may have an exit interview.
> **b** No, your company should do this for you.
> **c** Out of politeness, yes.
> **d** You don't have to say why you are leaving, you could just cite 'personal reasons' if you prefer.
> **e** It's a good idea to get a reference from your manager to help you get another job.
> **f** Yes, you should always put the fact that you want to leave in writing.
> **g** You shouldn't have to pay any money back to your employer unless you have been paid in advance for something.

2 Discuss this as a whole class.

> **Answers**
> You should do 'f' before any of the others, but otherwise the order doesn't matter.

3 Put learners in groups of three and give each group a set of the nine paragraphs. Ask learners to arrange them to form three emails. In feedback, give each learner the bottom half of the worksheet showing the answers.

4 Ask learners to discuss the questions in their groups.

> **Answers**
> **a** Svetlana is writing to ask for a reference; Rani is writing to say she has decided to leave her job; Sung Lee is writing to say goodbye to her colleagues.
> **b** Mr Khan was Svetlana's IT teacher; Mrs Selassie is Rani's manager; 'everyone' refers to Sung Lee's colleagues.

5 Ask learners to do this question alone and then discuss this as a whole class.

> **Answers**
> Svetlana = formal (no abbreviations; 'As you will remember'; 'I wonder if you would be prepared to')
> Rani = formal (no abbreviations; 'I am writing to let you know that'; 'Yours sincerely')
> Sung Lee = informal ('Hi everyone'; abbreviations; 'if you'd like to meet up'; 'hoping to see some of you' instead of 'I am hoping to see some of you'; 'Cheers')

6 Ask learners to work in pairs to do this task. Explain that the phrases in italics are not wrong, but that the phrases in the boxes are more common ways of saying the same thing.

> **Answers**
> **1** a drink to say goodbye   **2** using this chance
> **3** leave this job   **4** says I need to
> **5** leave this job and start a new one
> **6** do a reference

7 Ask learners to work alone and choose one of the three emails to reply to (or see Extension below).

Extension
If you feel it is appropriate for your learners and their work situation, ask them to imagine that they have decided to leave their job. Tell them to write two emails in connection with this. They need to decide who to write to, and what the purpose of each email is.

Links to other themes in this book
For more on emails, see 10b and 15a.

> **Answers: Self-study exercises**
> **1** 1 induction day 2 refer to something 3 get by
>   4 resign 5 take the opportunity
> **2** 1 for 2 in 3 for 4 back 5 in 6 to

1 When you leave a job do you have to

a go for an exit interview?
b inform the Inland Revenue?
c tell your colleagues you are leaving?
d tell your employer why you're leaving?

e ask your manager for a reference?
f write a resignation letter?
g pay any money back to your employer?

2 Is it important to do these things in any particular order?

3 Your teacher will give you nine cards. Arrange them into three separate emails.

4 Read the emails and discuss these questions.

a Why are Rani, Svetlana and Sung Lee writing?
b Who are Mr Khan, Mrs Selassie and 'everyone'?

5 How formal are the three emails? Find examples of formal or informal language in each.

6 Improve the emails by replacing the underlined phrases in the text with the phrases below.

1 farewell drink   2 taking this opportunity   3 hand in my notice   4 stipulates
5 move on   6 act as a referee

Emails for task 3

Dear Mr Khan,
As you will remember, I was in your IT class last year. I am writing to ask you a personal favour.

Since leaving college, I have been working in a supermarket, but have decided that it is time to _leave this job and start a new one_. I am looking for a job where I can use my IT skills, and I wonder if you would be prepared to _do a reference_ for me.

I would be grateful if you could let me know if you would be able to do this, and if so, if you would be happy for me to put your phone number and email address on my CV.
I look forward to hearing from you, and thank you very much in advance for your help.
Best regards,
Svetlana Raskolnikov

Dear Mrs Selassie,
I am writing to let you know that I have decided to _leave this job_. I have enjoyed working here, but for personal reasons, I would like to leave.

I would like to finish on the 31st of next month. This is slightly more than the one month's notice that my contract _says I need to_.

Could you please let me know if there are any formalities I need to know about in connection with my final few weeks at work? I look forward to hearing from you.
Yours sincerely,
Rani Patel

Hi everyone,
As you might know, this Friday's going to be my last day here.

That's why I'm _using this chance_ to say goodbye to you all. I've had a great two years working here, and there are lots of people I'll really miss.

So, if you'd like to meet up before I leave, I'll be going to the pub opposite the main entrance, 'The Happy Lion'. It'd be lovely if you could join me for a _drink to say goodbye_.
Anyway, hoping to see some of you on Friday.
Cheers, and all the best in the future, Sung Lee

16b Entrepreneurs

Type of activity
Jigsaw reading about individuals who have started or developed a business; answering comprehension questions; role play. Individual and pair work.

AECC reference
Rt/E3.4a; Sc/E3.4c; Rt/L1.5a; Sc/L1.3b

Aims
To develop reading and speaking skills.

Vocabulary
get things off the ground, venture, instalments, cash flow, take something forward, stay in touch, make a contact, word of mouth, drop someone a line

Preparation
Photocopy one worksheet for each learner.

Photocopy and cut up one worksheet for every four students, in order to give each learner either Text A, B or C for the jigsaw reading.

Differentiation
Stronger learners: ask them to read more than one text for task 1 and ask them to identify other useful vocabulary.

Weaker learners: omit task 4.

Warmer
Ask the learners if they have ever thought about starting a business of their own, or if they know someone who has. Talk about what might be difficult when starting a business.

1 Elicit the word *entrepreneur*, and tell the learners they are going to read about one. Give each learner a card (A, B or C) and ask them to read it and prepare to tell other students about what they have read. To help them summarise, ask them to try and identify the main key advice the entrepreneur is giving. Check answers individually before moving on to the next stage.

> **Answers**
> **A** Limit costs and do some work for free at the start.
> **B** Put thought into a good business plan.
> **C** Meet and tell as many people as you can about your business.

2 Make new groups of three so that each group contains at least three learners who have read a different text. Each learner should summarise the text they read and share the main piece of advice. Encourage questions and discussion.

3 Hand out the worksheets. Ask the groups to choose the best title for each text, but discourage them from reading the other texts at this stage. Do not check answers until after task 4.

4 Ask learners to read the other texts to check that they agree with the title.

> **Answers**
> **1** A **2** C **3** B

Extension
Set up role-play interviews between a journalist and one of the three entrepreneurs. Allow learners to decide if they would like to be a journalist or entrepreneur, and which entrepreneur they would like to interview or be. Allow three to five minutes for the learners to prepare what they will say in groups. To do this, put all the learners playing the role of the journalist interviewing Phil into one group. Do the same for the other characters.

Additionally, ask learners to do a research project, in which they find out about a recently started business in their town and present a profile of the business and/or the entrepreneur to their colleagues. If possible, arrange for the learners to plan and conduct interviews with the business person.

> **Answers: Self-study exercises**
> **1** 1 a 2 e 3 d 4 c 5 b
> **2** 1 monthly installments 2 Chamber of Commerce 3 cash flow 4 business partner 5 business plan

1 Your teacher will give you a text about a successful business. Read it and prepare to summarise it for your group.

2 In your group, summarise the text you read.

3 Choose the best title (1–4) for each article.

  1 How I started our business without much money
  2 How I make contacts for my business
  3 How I developed our business strategy

4 Now read the other three texts. Did you choose the best titles?

Texts for task 1–4

A

Phil Cavalier-Lumley

My business partner, Mark, and I were confident there was a market for our video production business. To get things off the ground, most of what we did involved borrowing. We needed to make a demo video first, so we borrowed some cameras and filmed someone's wedding without charging them*. We had to pay for the tapes, but I already had a computer, so we got some free software and this enabled us to edit the tapes. The results weren't fabulous, but at least now we could say to people that we did wedding videos. It was very much a part-time venture and we didn't take a wage – we both had other full-time jobs. I used my own car to get to jobs, which I didn't charge to the business. I used my computer to design some flyers and I photocopied a load off. We got a few jobs as a result. We also placed an ad in *Yellow Pages*. They allowed us to pay in monthly instalments of about £60, which helped with cash flow. The ad generated loads of work.

*without asking them to pay anything

B

Prashad Restaurant

Mum and Dad opened the shop 13 years ago, selling Indian sweets and Bombay mixes. They always had ideas about the future, and the business was doing well, but they never had a business plan – they didn't see the need. But without a business plan, they lacked a sense of where the business was at and how best to take it forward. I'd just finished a business studies degree and returned to work for the family business. I asked Mum and Dad what they wanted to do – keep going as they were or take things forward. The shop's turnover had been declining slowly for a few years. Something had to be done. The food we produce is superb. Mum really is a fabulous cook, of that there's no question. So we decided to make more of her skills by opening a small restaurant with 25 seats, which is what we eventually did, and Prashad opened last year. I knew that having a well thought-out business plan would be essential.

C

Sarah Thomas

A lot of the work I've done since starting my business in 2004 has resulted from networking*. One of the first things I did was to join my local Chamber of Commerce, and I've been to lots of their meetings, trade shows and conferences. They are a good way of meeting people. Speak to people in a friendly way and listen. It's not just a question of how someone can help you, but also how you can help them. Don't forget that the people you meet may recommend you to someone else. Word of mouth is the best form of advertising. Once you've made a contact, stay in touch. When you get back home after the event, drop them a line, saying how nice it was to meet them, and that you hope you'll meet again.

* meeting and speaking with people who can be useful to you in your work

16c Business start-up

Type of activity
Role play; learners negotiate the terms of a bank loan to start up a new business. Group work.

AECC reference
Sd/E3.1b; Lr/E3.5b; Sd/L1.1b; Lr/1.2b

Aims
To develop speaking and negotiation skills.

Vocabulary
set up a business, loan, invest, target market, unique selling point, payment holiday, appointment, risk, interest, competitive, arrangement fee

Preparation
Photocopy one worksheet for every two learners and cut these into Learner A's half and Learner B's half.

If possible, arrange the classroom furniture in a way which will enable bank staff to be based at a desk, and business people to walk around and browse, looking for the best offer.

Differentiation
In setting up the role play, be aware that some learners may not be so familiar with the notions of loans, repayment terms, interest rates and arrangement fees, so be prepared to explain this. You may wish to allocate roles (entrepreneurs or bankers) according to the personalities, interests or real-world experience of the learners.

Warmer
Ask learners what kind of things people may need to borrow money for, whether for personal or business use. Explain that they are going to take part in negotiations where business people are trying to arrange a loan. Learners could watch a clip from the BBC series *Dragon's Den* if you can access one on the Internet. This is a reality TV show in which real-life entrepreneurs pitch to a panel of investors in order to secure the finance their business needs. Ask learners what sort of business they would start if money was no object. Use responses from this question to inform your decision about who is given the role of the entrepreneurs for the role-play activity.

1 As learners may not be familiar with the idea of loans, arrangement fees, etc. present them with the following imaginary scenario:

Explain that you need to borrow £10 until the end of the week. Your brother and sister have both offered to help you, but they are very strict about the terms and conditions.

Your brother will lend you the £10, but will charge you £1 per day (in interest) until you pay him back.

Your sister does not intend to charge you any interest, but says that she will make you pay a one-off fee of £5 for any loan.

Discuss the pros and cons of both loans, and ask learners to say who is offering you the better deal. Then explain that this is essentially how banks operate with loans: the brother's £1 in interest would be a daily interest rate of 10 per cent (banks usually have a yearly or per annum rate), and the sister's £5 fee would be equivalent to the arrangement fee.

2 Explain that they are going to negotiate the terms of a loan, in order to start up a business. Give half the learners the Entrepreneur role card, and the other half the Business development manager role card. Ask small groups of entrepreneurs to work together to plan what they are going to say; and small groups

of business development managers to work together to plan their questions. Make sure that the business development managers choose the terms of their loans individually and fill in the loan summary sheet as they see fit. Monitor, and check that all pairs are able to come up with suitable ideas.

3 After about 20 minutes, ask the business development managers to sit at different desks (representing the different banks they work for) around the room. Explain that the entrepreneurs should go and talk to several different banks to find the best offer of a loan. Encourage learners to try and negotiate better deals for themselves – this is what can bring humour to the activity.

Extension
Ask learners to check the websites of real high-street banks to find out what business loans are available, and feed back to the group about which one is best and why.

Links to other themes in this book
For more on numeracy, see 9b, 15b and 15c.

Answers: Self-study exercises

1 unique selling point; target market; set up a business; negotiate a loan; business plan

2 1 set up a business 2 target market
  3 unique selling point 4 business plan
  5 negotiate a loan

Rolecards

✂︎ ⟨

Student A: Entrepreneur

You would like to set up your own business. To do this, you need a loan from the bank. You are about to go to some meetings with the business development managers from some high-street banks, who will want to know as much as possible about you and your business. You need to be able to tell them in detail about the following:

- the business you want to start
- your experience in this industry
- the amount of money you can invest
- the amount you need to borrow
- what you propose to spend this on
- your target market
- your business's unique selling point.

Think of any other questions you want to ask the business manager, and write them here.

Can I take payment holidays?

_____

_____

_____

_____

Student B: Business development manager

You are the business development manager at a high-street bank. Today, you have appointments with several people who want loans to set up their own businesses. This is a great opportunity for the bank (you earn a lot of money from these loans), but it is also a risk (you do not want to lend to someone who will go bankrupt before repaying the loan). In your interview, you want to find out:

- what experience the person has
- how likely the person's business is to succeed
- how safe it will be for your bank to lend to this person.

Discuss with your colleagues what questions you will ask your prospective customers, and write the questions here.

Could you tell me what you were doing before you decided to set up your own business?

_____

_____

_____

Now work alone. Look at the information from your bank's website, which you will use during your meetings to find the right loan for the customer. Choose a name for your bank, and then complete the information in the table. Remember – you need to be competitive in order to win business!

.... Bank

COMPARE LOANS

Loan type	Amount	Rate of interest	Loan term	Arrangement fee	Payment holidays? (Y/N)
Small loan	From £500 to £..............	...............% per annum	From 6 months to .... years	£..............	....
Large loan	From £.............. to £	...............% per annum	From .... to	£..............	....

Self-study exercises

1a Your CV

1 Choose the correct answer.

1 When you are inviting someone to sit down, what do you say?
a Take a seat. b Make a seat.
2 What do people say to show that something is their honest opinion?
a To be honest b Being honest
3 Why do people use the phrase 'fair enough'?
a To say that something is reasonable. b To say that something is true.
4 If someone says that something is 'a long story', they mean that it is
a boring. b complicated.
5 What is another way to say 'definitely not'?
a No method! b No way!

2 Complete the sentences with a phrase from task 1.

1 What? You expect me to wash all those dishes, while you just sit and watch TV? ....*No way!*............ .
I did it last time, so it's your turn.
2 Hello. Lovely to meet you. Come right in and .... Can I get you a coffee or something?
3 How did I meet my wife? Well, it's .... actually. But basically we both happened to be on holiday in Berlin at the same time. And we ended up on the same train.
4 Well, if you want my opinion, ... , I think it's just too expensive.
5 So, you want to meet in my office this week, your office next week, mine the week after and so on? Alright? That sounds .... So I'll see you on Thursday.

1b Job hunting

1 Choose the correct preposition.

1 I'm applying for / on work as a security guard.
2 I've sent off / down several job applications this week, so now I'm keeping my fingers crossed.
3 The interview went really well – I think I'm in with / by a good chance.
4 I like the people who work there, and I reckon I'd fit on / in really well.
5 I went in / through the whole newspaper today, and there wasn't a single job ad I liked.

2 Match the sentence halves to make definitions of the words and phrases in italics.

1 The section in your CV where you give a summary of yourself
2 You explain why you are suitable for a job in
3 A *strong candidate*
4 Your *dream job*
5 The feeling of not knowing what to write

a is the job that you would really love to do.
b is called your *personal profile*.
c is known as *writer's block*.
d a *covering letter*.
e is someone who has a good chance of getting the job.

1c Get online

1 Look at the sets of collocations. In each set, cross out the one which is not a real collocation.

1 search computer	search engine	search results
2 current vacancies	vacant vacancies	job vacancies
3 speculative job	speculative application	speculative enquiry
4 job application	job employment	job title

2 Complete the sentences with a phrase from task 1.

1 Even if the company isn't advertising any jobs at the moment, why don't you just submit a ..*speculative application*..., and hope for the best?
2 My .... is actually 'Warehouse Operative'. At least, that's what it says on my contract. But I just tell people I'm a forklift truck driver.
3 Google is the best known .... in the world.
4 If you Google something, you normally get about ten .... on your screen at one time.

2a The language of recruitment

1 Match the words to make phrases from unit 2a.

maternity — -related pay
stock — date
closing — cover
performance — range
salary — phrases

2 Complete the sentences with a phrase from task 1.

1 Job ads always seem to consist of the same .... *stock phrases* .... like 'team player', 'attractive package'.
2 I've got a fixed-term post doing .... for someone whose baby is due next week.
3 They're planning to introduce .... soon, which is great for me, because I should be getting loads extra on commission.
4 I can't come out tonight – I'm doing a job application, and the .... is tomorrow.
5 The .... for the post is from £18,600 to £21,730.

2b Job adverts

1 Complete the job adverts with the abbreviations from the box.

| ~~pa~~ | CRB | K | IT |

1
> **Oaklands school is looking for catering staff for our busy school kitchen.**
>
> Looking for a part-time job (14 hours during term-time)?
> Want to earn £9,500 ___*pa*___?
>
> All applicants will need to complete a _____ check. This is to ensure a safe environment for our children.

2
> **Could you work in telesales?**
>
> Do you have strong _____ skills?
> Join a fab team – and earn up to £28 _____ annually.
> Contact Jason@gosales.co.uk.

2c Applying in writing for a job

1 Complete the crossword

Across

2 Work as an au pair, babysitter or nursery teacher is known as c.................... work. (9)
4 Remember to a.................... your CV when you send your application by email. A lot of people forget this, so always check it's there before you click 'send'. (6)
6 Ability to use a computer: I....................
   s.................... (2, 6)
7 The ability to interact well with people: c.................... skills. (13)

Down

1 It's always a good idea to include the j.................... r.................... number when you send a job application. The job ad usually tells you what this is. This helps the agency or employer know which job you are applying for. (3,9)
3 It's better to write a c.................... application than a long-winded one. (7)
5 Another word for a job: p.................... (8)

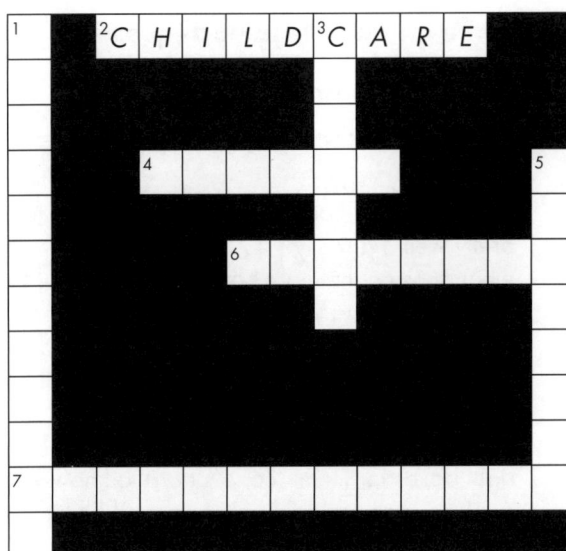

3a Interview tips

1 Complete the sentences by using the correct form of the verbs in the box.

ask	~~find out~~	answer	make	get	relax

1 Start .... *finding out* .... about the company well before the interview.
2 It's not a bad idea to film or record yourself .... questions when you practise the interview.
3 Allow yourself enough time .... to the interview room.
4 Remember that you don't get a second chance .... a good first impression.
5 .... about the pay too early in an interview is considered rude.
6 In the interview, just try .... and be yourself.

2 Choose the correct word.

1 I always try and (anticipate) / *forecast* what questions they are likely to ask me in an interview.
2 As a rule of *finger / thumb*, I think of three things I want to ask the interviewer at the end of the interview.
3 I find it helpful to take a copy of my CV to refer *from / to* if I need to refresh my mind about what I have done and when.
4 When they ask me about my current job, I try to be *affirmative / positive* about it, even though the truth is that I can't stand it!

3b At the interview

1 Find and correct the four grammatical mistakes in this set of interview questions.

1 How many hours ~~do usually you~~ work per week? *do you usually*
2 What have you learnt from your current job?
3 Why have you decided look for another job?
4 What is it about this job most appeals to you?
5 How would your current boss describe you?
6 How much experience of dealing with the public you have had?
7 Can you give an example of a time when have you worked effectively in a team?
8 Please explain how you feel you meet the requirements of the successful applicant, as set out in the job description.

2 Write an answer to each question.

3c After the interview

1 Choose the correct word (a, b or c) to complete the email.

Hi Bob,

Guess what – I had an interview yesterday for my dream job, working in an art gallery! Think it went pretty well. I'd really (1) ....*done*........ my homework this time and found out about the gallery and what goes on the night before the interview. I'd read quite a bit about some of the main artists who exhibit there and was able to talk about them because the information was still (2) .... in my memory.

It was weird – I was actually more excited than nervous before the interview, and I really wanted to show them I would be a good (3) .... player. Anyway, it seemed to go OK. I think I (4) .... a pretty good account of myself really. I just hope I (5) .... all the right boxes for them, 'cos it's hard to know what sort of person they really want.

Anyway, I should find out soon, and I'll let you know how I get on.

Best wishes,

Hai

1 a made	b (done)	c taken
2 a clear	b new	c fresh
3 a group	b team	c gallery
4 a had	b got	c gave
5 a ticked	b filled	c completed

From *English at Work* © Cambridge University Press 2011 **PHOTOCOPIABLE**

4a Chatting with colleagues

1 Put the conversation in the right order.

1 Nothing much, I just put my feet up.
2 Alright then, see you around.
3 Hi, how's it going?   1
4 Brilliant actually, yeah. Went to a party. What did you get up to?
5 Sounds great. I'm shattered now – I think that's what I'll be doing next weekend. Anyway, catch you later.
6 Not bad thanks. Good weekend?

2 Which informal phrases in the conversation mean

1 I relaxed   *I just put my feet up*
2 What did you do?
3 very tired
4 goodbye (x2)

4b Modern job titles

1 Here are some more job titles. Match the job titles with the descriptions.

1	Administrative Assistant	a	checks that cars are working properly
2	Air Cabin Crew Member	b	is a secretary
3	Data Entry Operator	c	makes things for dentists
4	Dental Laboratory Technician	d	is also known as a Flight Attendant
5	Food Counter Attendant	e	puts information onto a computer
6	Human Resources Scheduler	f	keeps things clean
7	Hygiene Operative	g	arranges the times when people work
8	Large Goods Vehicle Driver	h	helps children get to school safely
9	Machine Operator	i	writes computer programs
10	Revenue Protection Officer	j	fills supermarket shelves
11	Software Developer	k	sells meat, fish, cheese, etc. in a supermarket
12	Stock Replenishment Executive	l	drives a lorry
13	Vehicle Maintenance Technician	m	works in a factory
14	School Road Crossing Assistant	n	checks that everyone has bought a ticket (e.g. on a bus)

4c Company structure

1 Find and correct the mistakes in the following text.

I work for a company called Air Meals, and we do all the in-flight meals for airlines at one of Britain's busiest airports. It was founded in 1978 by Morris Aleen, and he's still the COE (Chief Executive Officer). It's quite a large company, and employs 129 staffs.

But we're not all cooks. The firm is divided into three main ~~compartments~~. *departments* Each is run by one of the three senior managers who report directly at Mr Aleen. Joe Growley manages the Operations department. He is responsible of dealing with the airlines. Kathleen Howey is at charge of Marketing. The third manager is Jeanette Fleurette who manages the Catering department. She's my line manage.

2 Match the sentence halves.

1	People at the same level	a	to isn't here this week.
2	It must be difficult to line	b	Team have weekly meetings.
3	I need to meet with my line	c	manager for my annual appraisal.
4	The manager I usually report	d	manage someone you don't get on with.
5	The whole Senior Management	e	title, but exactly the same pay as before!
6	I've now got a better-sounding job	f	of seniority are usually on roughly the same salary.

5a Agency work

1 Read the text quickly. What is its purpose?

Are you looking for work?

Then look no further. Our Job: Your Job is one of the UK's largest agencies. We can find the right job for you.

for
- We do not charge you finding you a job.
- With us, there won't be any surprise deductions your monthly pay packet.
- All our partner firms will provide you with a copy your terms of employment.
- We ensure that all our partner firms comply UK employment law. You are entitled breaks – and you will receive them.

So what are you waiting for? Register with us now.

2 Correct the text by adding these prepositions in the right place.

from	of	~~for~~	to	with

5b Company policies

1 Complete the table with words in the same word families.

verb	adjective(s)	noun(s)
dismiss		1 *dismissal*
employ		2
	3	absenteeism, absence
	4	parent
5		evaluation
appraise		6

2 Complete the questions with words from task 1.

1 After how many days of ....*absence*........ do you need to get a doctor's note?
2 How often does your boss sit down with you formally to .... or
.... your performance?
3 Can all fathers take .... leave after their baby is born?
4 Do most of the .... at your work know the company policies?

5c Understanding an employment contract

1 Put the prepositions in the correct place to complete the email.

~~as~~	as	by	in	on	than	under	without

Hi Javier,
Guess what – I've just started a new job (1).............*as*............ a waiter. The people are nice, and
the work's fun. The thing is that the work is (2)............................. an 'as-and-when' basis, so I never
really know how many hours I'll do in any week. I just work (3)............................. required – I
actually did quite a lot last week (36 hours), but my employer is (4)............................. no obligation
to give me any work at all. So I'm expecting lots of days off!
The pay's not bad either – I get paid (5)............................. bank transfer (not in cash, like my
last job). And I'm paid (6)............................. arrears, but apparently I should get the money no
later (7)............................. the 5th of every month. The only thing is that I'm on probation, which
means they can sack me (8)............................. notice if I do anything really bad. So I'm on my best
behaviour!
See you soon,
Paddy

6a Danger! Understanding health and safety signs

1 Look at the health and safety signs and choose the right word or phrase.

1 You ~~mustn't~~/ *don't have to* light a match.
2 You *have to / can* wear ear protection.
3 You *are not allowed / are allowed* to walk this way.
4 You *must / could* wear boots here.
5 You *might / must* fall here.

6b Health and safety training

1 In the following text, the underlined words are in the wrong place. Move them to the right place in the text.

In the training today, they told us to make sure there are no wet floors (because otherwise someone
slip
might ~~scald~~ and hurt themselves). We were also told about precautions when handling hot things,
scald
because it's easy to ~~slip~~ yourself, and that can be really painful. Equipment left in the wrong place is
an accident *lying* to happen. So we need to always keep things out of harm's *safety*, and put things
away when not in use. We should never leave things *waiting* around. So far we've got an excellent
way record, with only two minor accidents in the last four years.

2 Find words and phrases in task 1 that mean

1 burn your skin — s.*cald*.....................
2 In a safe place — out of h.................... w....................
3 a dangerous situation — an accident w.................... to h....................
4 not put things away — leave things l.................... a....................
5 fall on a wet floor — s....................
6 number of accidents reported — s.................... r....................

6c Reporting accidents

1 Match the words to make phrases, and use them, in the correct form, to complete the sentences below.

witness — accident
report — the accident
by — the accident
accidents — happen

1 The .... at about 12.15 pm.
2 Don't forget to .... as soon as possible.
3 When writing an accident report, always mention anyone who
.... *witnessed the accident* ....
4 Nobody meant to start the fire, it happened ....

2 Find and correct the two spelling mistakes in each sentence.

supervisor   *occurs*
1 You need to tell your ~~supervizor~~ about any accident that ~~ocurs~~.
2 I suffered an ellectric shock, and felt quite shacken afterwards.
3 It is your responsibilty to report any acident at work.
4 A lot of injuries are sustaned on building sights.
5 I need to raport an insident that happened this morning.

7a Computer language

1 Choose the correct word.

1 It was an internal vacancy, and only advertised on the firm's *internet /* (*intranet*) so that only existing employees could apply.
2 I'm sorry – I can't remember my *log off / login* details. How can I get these?
3 I need to replace the *hard drive / mouse* inside my computer.
4 A *file / spreadsheet* can be anything from a Word document to a movie or song: in other words anything that you can save on a computer.
5 It looks as if I'm going to have to *crash / reboot* my computer to get it working again.
6 You always need to be careful disconnecting any *software / hardware* like a memory stick or digital camera.
7 We use a *software / database* for storing all our clients' details.

2 Match the sentence halves.

1 If you don't log off, then
2 Don't only save your files
3 All staff can access the client database
4 First you need to enter your username
5 I'm not able to uninstall the program myself – I'll have

a and your password.
b the next user can't log on.
c to ask an administrator to do it for me.
d when they're using the company's intranet.
e on the hard drive – put them on the server as well.

7b Computer maintenance

1 Find and correct the five spelling mistakes. What do the mistakes have in common?

Ah – what a day! My computer's been giving me a hard time. I couldn't ~~acces~~ the Internet for ages. *(access)*

Turned out someone had used my machine and then disconected it! Very irritating… And then a

program wouldn't start, so I had to uninstal it, then install it again, which took ages. Shouldn't I

just get a new computer? I hear you say. Well, not necesarily – I reckon these problems are just as

comon in new machines as in old ones.

2 Find and correct the mistakes in three of the following sentences.

1 ~~What do you want~~ to do is just restart your computer. *What you want*
2 All you need doing is double-click here.
3 What you can do is cut and paste the address.
4 One thing to try would be to check the volume.
5 It's always the idea to see if your colleagues have a solution.
6 You might want to just wait and see what happens when you restart.

7c IT helpdesk

1 Choose the correct phrase.

1 I've just had a *pop-up message / ~~pop-up notice~~* saying it won't let me open this document.
2 It says only someone with *admin rights / admin reasons* can open it.
3 I can't download the *attached document / enclosed document*.
4 It's easy to do – just *cut and stick / cut and paste* the address.
5 If you're having problems printing, check that your *ink levels / ink amounts* are OK.

2 Match the problem with the appropriate advice.

1 I'm not receiving any emails.
2 My computer has frozen.
3 I can't read the email I just printed out.
4 I don't have the right software to open this attachment.

a Send it to helpdesk.
b Delete some of your old emails.
c Change the ink cartridge.
d Restart your computer.

8a Case studies

1 Complete the table with words in the same word families.

verb	adjective	noun
legalise	legal / illegal	1 *legality*
	homosexual	2
recruit		3
	4	transsexualism
discriminate		5
	6	pregnancy

2 Complete the sentences with a word from task 1.
1 A business which helps people find jobs is called a ....*recruitment*.......... agency.
2 The UK has lots of laws forbidding any racial or sexual .... against people in the workplace.
3 A person who would like to be the opposite sex is known as ....
4 A person who is attracted to members of the same sex is ...., although the adjectives 'gay' (for a man) and 'lesbian' (for a woman) are more commonly used.

8b Disability Discrimination Act

1 Choose the correct form of each word.
1 A lot of people who are visually (impaired) / impairing carry a white stick.
2 Climbing stairs can be very difficult for people with *limited / limiting* mobility.
3 People of all ages need to use a *heard / hearing* aid.
4 Please be *advised / advising* that all staff are to attend Equal Opportunities training.
5 We will be *run / running* the training three times to enable everyone to attend.

2 Find and correct the six spelling mistakes in the text below.

                    opportunities
As an equal ~~oportunities~~ employer, Bakton Town Council is committed to giving everyone a fair

chance to work with us. If you apply for a job with us, we will ask on your appliccation form if you

have a disabilty (such as impared hearing, limited mobility, or any other condition covered by the

Disability Discrimnation Act). This is to ensure that all disabeld candidates who meet our criteria are

invited for interview.

8c Equal opportunities monitoring

1 Match the words to make phrases.

complete ————————— the form
promote   candidates
treat (something)   equal opportunities
shortlist   confidentially

2 Complete the text with phrases from task 1.

As part of our efforts to (1).., Shipton City Library invites all
candidates to (2)..............*complete the form*............... below. We are an equal opportunities
employer, and welcome applications from all sections of the community. The form asks you to
state your ethnicity, as well as your religion and any disabilities. This information is for monitoring
purposes only; the form will be detached from your application. Any information you provide will not
be used to (3)... Please be advised that Sheffield City Library
will (4).......................... your information ...., in accordance with the Data
Protection Act.

Self-study exercises

9a Talking big money

1 Choose the correct word.

1 I should get an *incremental / (increment)* of about £700 on my salary this year.
2 I was a new employee, and had to start at the bottom of the *payslip / pay scale*.
3 You need to make sure you get a *P45 / P60* when you leave an employer.
4 New employees sometimes have to pay *urgency / emergency* tax.
5 £298 was taken off my pay in *deducts / deductions* this month.
6 I still haven't received my *PAYE / payslip* for this month.
7 You'll get your P60 at the end of the *finance / financial* year.

2 Match the sentence halves.

1 I get an hourly
2 You'll get your P60
3 I pay nearly £100 in National
4 If I get an increment next year,
5 I asked if I could have an advance
6 My first payslip showed that I was paying

a Insurance contributions every month.
b after the end of the tax year in April.
c rate of £7.25, plus tips.
d I'll be on the highest point of the payscale.
e on my salary this month, as I'm buying a car.
f emergency tax, so my take-home pay was quite low.

9b Getting paid

1 Unscramble the anagrams to find words and phrases from unit 9b.

LOYLPAR   NI SARARER   IPPSYAL   NI NEACDAV   YPA AYD
PAYROLL

2 Complete the sentences with a word or phrase from task 1.

1 Please let us know ...., so that we have time to make arrangements.
2 I need to phone ....*Payroll*.......... and ask them about my tax code.
3 Payments are made .... by bank transfer.
4 I usually receive my .... by the 20th of the month.
5 I can't wait till .... – I'm running out of money.

9c Payment queries

1 Complete the extracts from the blog with the correct preposition.

1 I've just started work ....*at*............. a leisure centre.
2 ... they've told me I'm .... £36 a day for a 13-hour shift.
3 My employer is now three weeks late .... my salary payment this month.
4 They're just being unreasonable .... withholding money.
5 You should be getting .... least the National Minimum Wage.
6 ... even if you are right .... the bottom of the pay scale.
7 Your new employer then uses this to work .... how much you have to pay.
8 One piece of advice though – hang .... to all your payslips, because you might want to contact your local tax office.

2 Match the sentence halves to make definitions of the underlined words.

1 If something is a *real laugh*,
2 A *shift* is
3 If you are given a *deadline*,
4 You might ask for *an advance* if
5 If something is *confidential*,

a you need to do something before a fixed date or time.
b then it is really enjoyable.
c you need to receive some of your pay earlier than usual.
d a period of time when somebody works.
e it is private, and other people cannot / will not find out about it.

From *English at Work* © Cambridge University Press 2011   **PHOTOCOPIABLE**

10a Phoning in sick

1 Choose the correct spelling.

1 a spliting   b splitting *(circled)*
2 a headacke   b headache
3 a self-certify   b self-sertify
4 a absence   b absense
5 a consecutive   b consequtive
6 a disqualiffy   b disqualify
7 a doctors' note   b doctor's note
8 a faillure   b failure

2 Find and correct the mistakes in Alexey's return to work form.

RETURN TO WORK FORM *STRELNIKOV*

Surname (BLOCK CAPITALS) __Strelnikov__   Other names: ____Alexey____

Post Title _forklift operator_   Department ____warehouse____

Absence reported to ___Anne peters___ at ___2 March___ (time) on ____8:20____ (date)

First day of illness __March 2 Tues__   Last day of illness ___3 March___

First day of absence _____2/3_____   Date of return to work _Thurs 4 March_

Total number of days/shifts of absence on this episode ____2 day____

10b Dealing with customer complaints

1 Complete the email with a word from unit 10b. The first letter is provided.

Dear Mr Poddle,
With (1)r egard............................ to your email this morning, I am writing to offer my
(2)s....................................... apologies for the error this morning. I was
(3)c....................................... to hear that your customer, Mr Donizetti, flying from Milan Malpensa,
arrived at Aberdeen Airport to find that no car was waiting for him. I have been working hard to
(4)r....................................... the issue and establish what went wrong. We regret the inconvenience
caused to Mr Donizetti and to yourselves. As we very much value your (5)c.......................................
custom, we would like to offer the next two airport pickups for you free of charge as a gesture of
(6)g....................................... .
We hope that this will go some way towards making up for our (7)e.......................................
With apologies once again and best wishes,
Ali Khan
Manager, Aberdeen Cabs

10c Everyday problems

1 Find and correct the vocabulary mistakes in four of these sentences.

1 There's no sugar left – we've run off. *out*

2 The scanner's off order, but someone's coming in to fix it tomorrow.

3 Unfortunately, I can't come on June 19, because it clashes with some training

  I need to attend.

4 I'm really sorry. I didn't call them. I slipped my mind.

5 I've got to meet quite a tight deadline with this project, so things are a bit hectic.

6 Is there any chance you could stand out for me at work next Saturday? I want

  to go to a friend's wedding.

7 There's another meeting scheduled for tomorrow.

Self-study exercises

11a What's the law?

1 Match the names of the act (law) in the box with the summaries below.

| Disability Discrimination Act   Sex Discrimination Act   Equal Pay Act |
| Race Relations Act   Human Rights Act   Statutory Maternity Pay Regulations |

1 This law concerns fairness in recruitment, promotion and training. It makes it illegal to discriminate against someone because of their gender or marital status. *Sex Discrimination Act*

2 This law makes it unlawful to discriminate against someone because of their colour or ethnic/national origin. However, employers do still need to check whether a new employee is entitled to work in the UK.

3 This law means that people of both sexes should earn the same for doing similar work. Employers must treat men and women equally with regard to pay, as well as holidays and pension rights.

4 This law protects the rights of people with various conditions, including learning difficulties, impaired vision or hearing, and progressive conditions such as AIDS or multiple sclerosis. It means that employers should make their workplace an easy place for a disabled person to work in.

5 This legislation sets out a woman's entitlement to receive pay from her employer before and after her child is born.

6 This law protects people's right to freedom of thought and religious belief. It means that employers can't discriminate against applicants because of their sexual orientation, religion or family circumstances.

11b Annual leave

1 Match the phrases with the definitions.

1 *make do with* something   a   What you are allowed to have.
2 *prioritise* something   b   A problem when two events are happening at the same time.
3 a *clash*   c   treat something as urgent; do it sooner
4 *entitlement*   d   accept

2 Complete the sentences with a word or phrase from task 1.

1 I've got a timetable ....*clash*..........: my English class and my IT class are scheduled for Thursday at 11.20. What shall I do?

2 You've already used up your leave .... for this year, so if you do need more time off, then I'm afraid it'll have to be unpaid leave.

3 Unfortunately we've run out of milk, so we'll just have to .... that powdered stuff till we get some more.

4 I promise I'll .... those invoices and deal with them before I go home today.

11c Maternity and paternity leave

1 Choose the correct verb.

1 Do you know if I am (paying) / contributing National Insurance contributions?
2 I'm going to *make / take* my maternity leave later in the year.
3 She argued that she had *suffered / made* a detriment when they offered her fewer hours when she returned from maternity.
4 He *took / did* his claim for sex discrimination to the Employment Tribunal.
5 I should *get / make* two weeks off when my son is born.
6 My wife actually *took / gave* birth on the very first day of her maternity leave.

2 Choose the correct preposition to complete the sentences.

| for   under   of   from   of   from |

1 I'm not sure if I qualify ....*for*.......... paternity pay – how can I find out?
2 I don't think my employer is behaving reasonably .... the circumstances.
3 Maternity pay is paid for a maximum .... four weeks.
4 There is a lot of equal opportunities legislation which protects you .... suffering at work because of pregnancy.
5 I think all men can claim statutory paternity pay regardless .... how much they earn.
6 My brother was only absent .... work for two days after his son was born. Then he went back to work.

From *English at Work* © Cambridge University Press 2011 **PHOTOCOPIABLE**

12a Helping out

1 Complete the dialogue with the missing words. There is one word missing per line.

here	is	can	to	mind	╳	like	of	much

I

Customer:	Sorry, can just ask you something?
Shop assistant:	Yes, of course, how I help?
Customer:	I can't seem find the digital cameras.
Shop assistant:	OK, well what you want to do go to the main entrance, and they're on your left.
Customer:	Right. Would you showing me?
Shop assistant:	Sure. Would you to follow me?
Customer:	OK, that's very kind you.
Shop assistant:	No problem. We're to help.
Customer:	That's great. Appreciated.

12b A green workplace

1 Look at the sets of collocations. In each set, cross out the one which is not a real collocation.

1 coffee
~~kettle~~
mug
time

4 to chuck
to throw
to dispose
something in the bin

2 fake
greenery
fifty-pound note
mistake

5 disposable
razor
cup
recycling

3 to plug
to unplug
to plug in
the computer

2 Which of the phrases in task 1

1 can be made of polystyrene or plastic?
2 is a low-maintenance way of making a room look nicer?
3 is something you use to shave?
4 might you do when you leave your workplace to keep electricity costs down?
5 would you do to some rubbish that can't be recycled?
6 might be at around 11am? *coffee time*

12c Working outdoors

1 Match the words to make phrases.

building   vest
potential   lunch
high-viz   motoring law
champagne   employer
breach of   site

2 Complete the sentences with a phrase from task 1.

1 The company I work for is ten years old next week. So they're organising a ....
to celebrate! I can't believe it!
2 A golden rule is: remember that everyone you come across in your working life is a
.... So be nice to them – they might give you a job one day!
3 I'm a construction worker. At the moment, my work is on a large ......*building site*...... in the centre
of town.
4 For health and safety reasons, if anyone turns up for work without their helmet or
.... , they won't be allowed onto the site.
5 Nowadays, hardly any .... , from speeding to double parking, goes unnoticed.
There are CCTV cameras on every corner, and lots of traffic wardens about.

13a Qualifications in the UK

1 Write the qualifications next to the place where they are usually taken.

| A levels   GCSEs   degrees   PhDs   HNDs |

School: *A levels*
College:
University:

2 Complete the text with *the, a, an* or – (no article).

We're always hearing about (1).........*the*.......... value of qualifications, but I'm wondering whether it's all just (2)........................ myth. Take my friend Paul for (3)........................ example. Paul's from (4)........................ really well-qualified family – his parents both have (5)........................ PhDs. His brothers and sisters all have (6)........................ diplomas and at least one degree each. Paul's really bright, and he knew he wanted to work in (7)........................ software development even when he was (8)........................ little boy. But he taught himself, and didn't go to (9)........................ university. And at 17, he'd found himself (10)........................ really well-paid job in (11........................ IT. I asked him (12)........................ other day if he's glad he left (13)........................ full-time education so young. After all, it didn't do him any harm! And he said no – he thinks he was just lucky, but that everyone should get (14)........................ benefits of (15)........................ good university education!

13b Exam task practice

1 Several words from this unit have two meanings. Look at the two definitions and choose which meaning is being used in the sentence in *italics*.

1 Exercise: *I understand that there is a 14-day cooling-off period on your services. As such, I wish to exercise my right to do so.*
   a   to use something that you have the legal right to use
   b   to do sport and physical activity to keep fit
2 Outstanding: *The balance became due on June 16, and is still outstanding.*
   a   something which has not been dealt with, or a payment which has not yet been made
   b   excellent
3 Settle: *You normally have 28 days to settle any invoice.*
   a   stop moving and stay in one place
   b   pay a bill
4 Quarter: *Things have been very quiet over the last quarter.*
   a   25 per cent; one of four equal parts
   b   a period of three months
5 Measures: *We need to take measures to reduce our spending.*
   a   units which show size, weight, distance, etc.
   b   things done in order to achieve a purpose

2 Complete the sentences with a word from task 1 in the correct form.

1 As a precautionary ....*measure*........ , we've installed CCTV cameras in the car park.
2 He's a good manager on the whole, but I don't think he's very good at .... authority.
3 We're expecting business to pick up in the second .... after a slow start to the year.
4 We'd be very grateful if you could .... the balance as soon as possible.
5 There are a couple of .... issues that we still need to sort out before we go home today.

13c Evaluating a student's exam performance

1 Find and correct the four prefix or suffix mistakes in these sentences.

1 My partner is a better ~~negotiationer~~ *negotiator* than me, so she deals with contracts and payments. I'm too soft!
2 We're expecting a deliverment of equipment from our supplier some time this morning.
3 I do hope the delay will not cause you any inconvenience. Please accept our apologies.
4 He was suspended for making an unappropriate remark to a customer.
5 We export all over the world – at the moment I'm dealing with a shipment of goods to Ecuador.

2 Match the sentence halves.

1 I'm afraid I've been held   a   up for any problems you experienced due to our error.
2 As you are a valued customer   b   off all orders over £50.
3 Book now to receive 5%   c   up at work, and will be home about half an hour late.
4 I hope this makes   d   of ours, we'd like to make you a special offer.

From *English at Work* © Cambridge University Press 2011 **PHOTOCOPIABLE**

14a Telephoning

1 Which phrase do you think sounds more polite?

1 a (How can I help?)   b What do you want?
2 a Would you mind holding?   b Just wait, please.
3 a What's your reference number?   b Could I have your reference number, please?
4 a I'm afraid that's not possible.   b You can't do that.

2 Choose the correct word or phrase to complete the dialogue.

A: Hello? You're *up to /* (*through to*) Cozzie's.
B: Oh hello. Is *that / this* Cozzie's Bistro?
A: It is, yes. *That / This* is Dan *saying / speaking*. How can I help?
B: Oh, yes, I'm just calling to see if I can reserve a table for four for tonight.
A: Sure, just a moment. Can you hold the *line / phone* for a minute?
B: *Sure / Certain*.
A: OK, how does 7.30 *sound / appear*?
B: That's perfect, 7.30, yeah, great.
A: OK, and *what name was it / who are you*, please?
B: Khan, that's K-H-A-N.
A: Alright, so you've got a table for four booked for tonight at 7.30.
B: That's brilliant, thanks for your *help / helping*.
A: No problem, bye.

14b Service with a smile

1 Choose the correct answer: a, b or c.

1 What is a Hawaiian?
   (a a pizza)   b a cocktail   c a coffee
2 'I'll give you a shout' means
   a I'll be angry with you.   b I'll ask you a question.   c I'll let you know.
3 A £10-note can be described as
   a a tenner   b tennish   c a tenth
4 When a shop assistant says 'Have you got anything smaller?', they are talking about
   a money   b shopping bags   c food

14c Customer service Snakes and Ladders

1 Choose the correct answer.

1 Who or what can be described as elderly?
   a a building   (b a person)   c a book
2 If you wanted to ask someone to stop smoking a cigarette, you could ask them to
   a switch it off   b put it out   c keep it down
3 If you wanted to ask someone to make less noise, you could ask them to
   a switch it off   b put it out   c keep it down
4 Which word can be used with 'sorry' to mean 'very', as in 'I'm .... sorry'?
   a badly   b tragically   c terribly
5 To offer to help, you can say 'Would you like a ....?'
   a hand   b head   c back
6 Which of the following is part of a car?
   a the boot   b the shoe   c the sock

2 Look at the pairs of sentences. Which one do you think sounds more polite?

1 a Look, you can't smoke here.
   (b Sorry, could I ask you not to smoke here please?)
2 a He's not here. Can I help?
   b He's not here. Is there any way I can help?
3 a I'm afraid we're closed.
   b Sorry. Closed.

15a Email or snail mail?

1 Match the words and phrases with the definitions.

1 Your _inbox_ ...   d
2 _Snail mail_ ...
3 To _upload_ something ...
4 _Proof of postage_ ...
5 To _enclose_ something ...
6 You _attach_ a file (e.g. a document or photo) ...
7 You use a _postbox_ ...
8 A _draft_ of a document ...

a is a receipt from the Post Office that shows you sent something.
b is a humorous phrase that means using the postal service.
c means to make a file available on the Internet.
d is the part of your email account where emails to you are kept.
e to post letters.
f means to put it into a packet or envelope to send someone.
g is a version of the document before it is finished or finalised.
h when you want to send it with an email.

2 Complete the sentences with a word or phrase from task 1.

1 The best way to share photos with friends is to ...._upload_......... them to a web site.
2 Use a padded envelope if you want to .... anything heavy.
3 Sorry – I forgot to .... the contract in my last email. So here it is now (I hope!)
4 I do everything by email these days, and only use .... for sending birthday cards!
5 My .... is full, so I'm not receiving any new emails. I need to delete some.
6 Remember to get .... from the post office, in case your package goes missing.
7 Please find attached a first .... version of our agreement. Please let me know if you are happy with it, and I will post you a hard copy to sign.
8 There's a .... right outside my front door, which is handy for posting letters.

15b Getting it right

1 Look at the numbers. In each group, two are the same, and one is different. ~~Cross out~~ the one that is different.

1 a five quid	b a fiver	~~c five bucks~~
2 a £9.99	b nine nine nine	c nine ninety nine
3 a 2K	b two grand	c two pounds
4 a 0166 988 444	b oh one double six, nine eight, eight four, double four	c oh one double six nine triple eight double four
5 a 3/1	b March the first	c the first of March

15c Checking details

1 Find and correct the five mistakes in the email.

Hi Alan,
I'm just writing ~~checking~~ _to check_ the details about your visit next week, as I think there might have been a bit of a mix-out about the dates. I understood that you are coming next Friday (the 25th), but this doesn't correspond with what Fatima has in her diary. She has it down as Thursday the 24th, so clearly one of us, either myself or Fatima, has unaccurate information. Could you possibly just double-verify when you are going to be here, and let us know? That would be greatly appreciated.
Please accept our apologies for the disunderstanding, and we look forward to hearing from you soon, and seeing you here at AKRN next week.
With best wishes,
Jozef
Jozef Krampl
Senior Customer Development Executive, AKRN

16a Moving on

1 Which word or phrase is the odd one out?

1 farewell drink	leaving party	(induction day)
2 refer to something	provide a reference	act as a referee
3 move on	get by	change jobs
4 resign	stipulate	require
5 hand in notice	take the opportunity	write a letter of resignation

2 Choose the correct preposition from the box to complete the sentences.

in	for	for	back	to	in

1 I've decided to leave ....for.......... personal reasons.
2 I handed in my notice well .... advance, so that they had plenty of time to find a replacement.
3 The vacancies page in the local newspaper is a good place to look .... a job.
4 I'd taken an advance on my salary so when I left, I had to pay some money ....
5 I plan to stay in touch with my colleagues, and hope I'll continue to see them .... the future.
6 My new job starts on Monday, and I'm really looking forward .... it.

16b Entrepreneurs

1 Match the phrases with the definitions.

1 cash flow		a	amount of money coming into and leaving your business
2 business plan		b	group of business people from different companies
3 business partner		c	regular payments
4 monthly instalments		d	person you start a company with
5 Chamber of Commerce		e	document describing how a business is going to develop

2 Complete the sentences with a phrase from task 1.

1 Can I pay in ......monthly instalments......?
2 I go to monthly meetings organised by the local ....
3 We're having problems with .... , so might need a loan.
4 I don't always agree with my .... about how we should run our business.
5 We're developing our .... to see how we can expand in the future.

16c Business start-up

1 Match the words to make phrases.

unique	plan
target	selling point
set up	a business
negotiate	market
business	a loan

2 Complete the text, using phrases from task 1.

I was working as a nanny and live-in French teacher for an English family in London, but I was bored and I wanted a new challenge. So I decided to (1) .... finding French-speaking nannies for other families. Lots of parents want their children to learn French, so there was a massive (2) .... right here in my neighbourhood.
There were lots of other nanny agencies, but none of them combined childcare and education. This would be the only one, so it would have a (3)..............unique selling point.............. , and I was convinced it would work.
Starting a business is more expensive than you expect. I explained my
(4)........................... to the bank, and and managed to
(5)........................... so that I could buy a computer and rent a small office.
But anyway, I definitely think that starting my own business is the best thing I've ever done.

Audioscript

1a Your CV
Track 2

Orhan: Hello. Are you Julian?

Julian: Yes, hello, you must be Orhan. Come on in, take a seat, and let's look at your CV.

Orhan: Thank you. I emailed it to you actually. Did you get it?

Julian: I did, yes, and I've got a copy of it here.

Orhan: Oh good. So, is it alright?

Julian: Oh yes, definitely, it should help you get your first job. But the thing is, it's always good to keep coming back to your CV and updating it. A lot of people think that once they've written it, that's it.

Orhan: So, you think I should add to it, make it longer?

Julian: Well, I didn't say that. It's got to be concise. Yours is fine, not too long. And you've obviously proofread it carefully – I didn't find any mistakes, you know, grammar, spelling, punctuation. You'd be surprised how many CVs are full of mistakes.

Orhan: Oh right. Yeah, well actually, I got my mum to check it with me. She did find a couple of little things actually.

Julian: Right, well, better that she found them than a prospective employer. And I see you've included a picture. You might want to get rid of that.

Orhan: I can change it.

Julian: To be honest, I wouldn't advise that. Remember, CVs often go to a recruiting agency, and then they send it on to possible employers. But not until they've removed all the photos.

Orhan: Right. So is that, like, for equal opportunities or something?

Julian: That's right. Oh, and your date of birth too, I think you could lose that. Er, right, I see here, under Personal profile, you've put 'Seeking a challenging position that offers professional growth'.

Orhan: Yeah, I know, it's good that, innit? Did you like that bit?

Julian: Well, to be honest, no. It's the kind of thing lots of people put, but, it's well, a bit vague. Doesn't really tell a prospective employer very much, does it? I mean, what sort of work do you want to do?

Orhan: I want to work with computer graphics, web design, that sort of thing.

Julian: OK, well that needs to be clear. Just like under 'Interests and Achievements' you've just put football. But you play in the college team, don't you?

Orhan: Goalkeeper, yeah.

Julian: OK, well put that. Gives them evidence, you see, that you like to do things with other people. Like with the charity work, you see, that's gonna make a good impression on anyone that reads it. You haven't just said, you know, 'I do charity work', but you've given detailed information about it, so, yeah, that's excellent.

Orhan: Right. Oh, and I just got my National Insurance number the other day. I'll put that on as well.

Julian: Mmm… To be honest, I probably wouldn't. I mean, you wouldn't put your bank details on your CV, would you?

Orhan: Bank details? No way!

Julian: Right, well the same goes for National Insurance numbers. I mean, that's private information, financial information about you.

Orhan: OK, fair enough, better it stays confidential then, innit?

Julian: I think so, yes. One other thing – there seems to be a gap in your CV. You mention school, then you started A levels at this college in 2009, didn't you?

Orhan: 2009, yeah.

Julian: But I can't seem to find anything about what you did for the two years before that.

Orhan: Yeah, well, it's a long story, but basically I had to go back to Turkey for a bit, in 2007, helping my family and stuff. Came back in 2009.

Julian: OK, so I think you could just mention that briefly, just so anyone reading the CV knows. You can put it under 'Additional Information'. And apart from that, I think it's fine. Just remember to review and update your CV every so often.

Orhan: Alright, well, thanks very much, you've been really helpful.

2b Job adverts
Track 3

A: Seen these job ads?

B: Yeah, I had a look earlier actually. Thought you might want to go for the driving one. That sort of work would be right up your street. It's what you were doing before, wasn't it?

A: Yeah, but I've had enough. Wouldn't go back to that sort of work. I was away from my family for days at a time. And now that I've got a little boy, well, I wanna be around him, watch him grow up! Got to think about the work-life balance, you know, don't want to be working all the time. No, that's it. No more driving for me.

B: Oh, right, so you want to make a new start. Time for a career change then, is it?

A: Yeah, that's right.

B: So which one do you like the sound of? What about the job as a trainer?

A: Oh no, no, I could never do that. I'm just not cut out for that kind of work. Stuck in the gym all day, no, that's my idea of torture!

B: Yeah, I know, I was joking actually. Can't really see you as a trainer somehow! Although, looking at you, people might think, 'Wow, look at him. I don't want to end up looking like that – I'd better go to the gym!'

A: Yeah, right. Very funny! Actually, I think the one for me would be the one as warehouse manager.

B: Oh, I see. Well, no offence, but you haven't got any relevant experience, have you?

A: Erm well (and no offence taken, by the way!) I haven't been employed in a warehouse, but, I've got all the transferable skills from my work with logistics.

B: Sorry?

A: When I was driving. Used to take stuff to warehouses all the time, so I know how they work. All useful transferable know-how. What about you?

3b At the interview
Track 4

Mark: Good morning. You must be Rosana.

Rosana: Yes, that's right. Rosana Orilla.

Mark: Come in and have a seat. My name's Mark Pondle – I'm the theatre manager, and this is Janet Hargreaves who works with me.

Rosana: Hello. It's good to meet you.

Janet: Nice to meet you, too.

Mark: So Rosana, Janet and I are going to ask you a few questions, and then you'll have an opportunity to ask us anything about the role.

Rosana: OK.

Mark: So, first of all, why are you interested in this job?

Rosana: Well, I think you should do the work that you enjoy. I enjoy working with people so I think I'll really like this job.

Mark: Right. And I see from your CV that you're currently working in a hotel as a receptionist.

Rosana: Yes, and it's been interesting. I've learned a lot about customer service, including how to deal with complaints effectively. And of course it's been great for my English.

Mark: Well, this role will involve speaking to the public a lot as well.

Rosana: Yes, and that's one of the things that attracts me to this job.

Janet: Right, Rosana. Have you always been passionate about theatre?

Rosana: Yes, I have. Even when I was at school I loved drama, and I've been interested ever since.

Mark: Obviously, English isn't your first language, although you speak it very well. But do you feel you'll be able to cope with the demands of the work, dealing with the public and so on, in English?

Rosana: Well in my last job I was dealing with the public all the time, and although my English wasn't perfect, I was always able to communicate with customers. And I've been attending English classes because I'd like to be able to speak even better.

Janet: I see. Now, Rosana, do you have any questions for us?

Rosana: Yes. Er, there were a couple of things I wanted to ask about actually. First …

3c After the interview
Track 5

Jo: OK, well that's the last interview of the morning, so shall we just have a quick chat about the three candidates we've seen while they're still fresh in our memories?

Don: OK, good idea. Did well, didn't they?

Jo: Yes, it's not going to be easy choosing between them. Shall we start with Niran? I was really impressed with the way he expressed himself.

Don: Very articulate, wasn't he? Nothing about English language qualifications on his CV, though.

Jo: Hmm, but, he answered the questions well on the whole. Gave a good account of his education and working background. And there was nothing he didn't know about computers.

Don: That's right. And he gave a very honest answer about his strengths and weaknesses. But what about when you asked him why he wants to work for us?

Jo: Mmm, he was a bit vague there, wasn't he? I wondered if he'd done his homework at all. He hardly knew anything about the company.

Don: Yes, I wondered about that. OK, well what about Angela then?

Jo: Yeah, I can imagine her fitting in really well. The others in the team would really take to her.

Don: Yes, and I think they'd all work well together. She certainly came across as that kind of person, didn't she? You know what did concern me, though?

Jo: Her motivation? Experience?

Don: That's just it – you wonder about her staying power, you know, having moved from job to job so many times.

Jo: You never know, do you? What about when the novelty has worn off? Will she be off again, looking for new experiences?

Don: That's the thing, isn't it? So, what about Daniel then?

Jo: Well, he certainly ticks a lot of the right boxes. Had a pretty comprehensive CV, didn't he?

Don: Apart from all the typos!

Jo: Oh yes! But seems to have achieved a lot in a short time in his current job.

Don: But there was just something about him though that, well … I wasn't sure. Quite a capable guy, but …

Jo: A bit of a know-it-all though, eh? Seemed to have a bit of an attitude? Can imagine him being a bit hard to line-manage.

Don: Yes, I got that impression, too. When he was answering the one about how his line manager would describe him—

Jo: Yes, reading between the lines, I thought 'oh well, there's no love lost there, then'.

4a Chatting with colleagues
Track 6

1 A: Hello, I'm Ali. It's nice to meet you.
   B: Right.

2 A: Excuse me, I'm new here. It's my first day actually. I'm looking for—
   B: Not now, I'm busy.

3 A: So what do you do in your job?
   B: Maintenance.
   A: Er… Ok, I see.

4 A: Some of us are going for a drink after work. Do you fancy coming?
   B: I don't drink.

5 A: So, anyway, how long have you worked here?
   B: Too long.
   A: Oh.

6 A: Sorry, what did you say your name is?
   B: I already told you, didn't I? People either forget my name, or they pronounce it wrong. It's really annoying.

7 A: Where did you use to work before you started here?
   B: I don't want to tell you.

Track 7

1 A: Hello, I'm Ali. It's nice to meet you.
   B: Hello Ali, how are you doing? I'm Robert, but most people just call me Bob. So, yeah, well, good to meet you Ali.

2 A: Excuse me, I'm new here. It's my first day actually. I'm looking for—
   B: Oh, hello. Look I'm really sorry, but I can't stop, you see, I'm late for a meeting. I'm really sorry.
   A Oh, OK, no problem, I'll ask someone else.

3 A: So what do you do in your job?
   B: Oh, well I do, like, maintenance for all the machines, so I need to check if they're all sort of working properly, you know, that kind of thing.
   A: Oh, OK, I see.

4 A: Some of us are going for a drink after work. Do you fancy coming?
   B: Oh, that's really kind of you. But I don't drink, so I never, er, go to pubs, you know. But thanks all the same.
   A: Alright, well I'll see you tomorrow then.
   B: Yeah, bye!

5 A: So, anyway, how long have you worked here?
   B: Oh, I think it's about five years now. But to tell you the truth, I'm kind of thinking of getting another job.
   A: Oh really? So are you looking?
   B: Well actually, I've got an interview next week.
   A: Oh great, well good luck!
   B: Yeah, thanks. But look, can you just keep it to yourself for now, because, you know, I don't want people to know …

6 A: Sorry, what did you say your name is?
   B: Oh, it's Concepción.
   A; co… Sorry, what?
   B: Concepción, well, that's my full name. But, you can just call me Conchi for short. Conchi.
   A: Conchi? Oh yeah, that's much easier for me to pronounce. Thanks.

7 A: Where did you use to work before you started here?
   B: Oh well, you know, here and there, various places really. Yeah. What about you?

5b Company policies
Track 8

Gabby: IMJC Personnel Department, Gabby speaking.

Ibrahim: Oh hello, er this is Ibrahim. I've just started working here. It's my first week actually.

Gabby: Oh yes, hello Ibrahim. You're coming over to Personnel next week for your induction, aren't you?

Ibrahim: That's right, yes. And I've got the letter here from Personnel, and it suggests I should have a look at the company's policies. Well, I'm on the Personnel webpage now, under Policies. But I've got some questions actually, er, do you have a few minutes?

Gabby: Sure. How can I help?

Ibrahim: Well, it's just that there are so many of these policies. I'm not sure what some of them mean, and, well, which ones I should read.

Gabby: Well, you definitely don't need to look at all of them. Let's see. I suppose a good one to start with is the Health and Safety Policy. We want to, well, make sure our employees know how to stay safe from day one.

Ibrahim: Right, yes, that sounds like a good one to start with, so, yeah, I'll have a look at that. What about Absenteeism? Should I take a look at that? I mean, if I'm off sick or something?

Gabby: Oh, right, no, no, you need the Sick Leave Policy for that, tells you who to contact and when. Definitely one to take a look at. No, the Absenteeism one, that's more for unauthorised absence.

Ibrahim: Er, sorry, what?

Gabby: Unauthorised absence, you know, when someone doesn't come to work when they should and they haven't told us why.

Ibrahim: Oh right, well, I'm certainly not intending to do that.

Gabby: Great. You probably don't need to read that then!

Ibrahim: OK, and I see you've got a Dismissals Policy, and a Redundancy Policy. But aren't they both basically the same?

Gabby: No, not at all. They're quite different. Redundancy is when you lose your job but it's not your fault, like if they have to make staff cuts. Dismissal, well that's when you're—

Ibrahim: sacked? Like, someone's done something really serious?

Gabby: That's it. But unless someone is actually threatened with redundancy or dismissal, they're not things you need to read up on.

Ibrahim: What about holidays and stuff?

Gabby: Yes, certainly worth taking a look at the Leave Policy, which tells you all about how to apply to take leave.

Ibrahim: OK, I see and it says 'including Compassionate Leave'. Well, my wife's expecting our first baby, you see, so does this include time off for new fathers?

Gabby: Oh congratulations! Well, the one to take a look at would be the Parental Leave Policy. Compassionate leave is when you need to take time off in difficult circumstances, like to go to a funeral, or because a close family member is seriously ill.

Ibrahim: Ah, I see. And what about appraisal? What does that mean?

Gabby: Right, yes, definitely one to look at. This is where your manager sits down with you and talks about how well you've been getting on.

Ibrahim: Like an evaluation then?

Gabby: Yes, exactly. Er, well, was there anything else?

Ibrahim: No, I don't think so. You've been very helpful, so thank you very much.

Gabby: No problem. You might need some of those other policies one day, so do feel free to drop me an email if you want to know what any of the others mean.

6b Health and safety training
Track 9

Ahem. Welcome to today's training. As you know, it's health and safety today. I'm going to be talking about three golden rules of health and safety: don't rush; put things away; and stop and check. These apply to all of you, wherever you work.

Track 10

Alright, so golden rule number one is don't rush. Don't rush. Now, I'm not saying we want you to take really long coffee breaks, or, you know, work really slowly! What we mean is, take the time to do things properly. So, you're in the kitchen, food in the oven's ready to come out, but you can't see the oven gloves. So what do you do? Think, oh it's OK, it's probably not too hot, I haven't got time to go and find the oven gloves, I'll just use my bare hands? Absolutely not. Even if it takes you another minute to do it, get those gloves! You don't want to burn yourself. And in the restaurant, I know it gets busy, but a waiter in a rush bringing four bowls of hot tomato soup, well, that's an accident waiting to happen. You could find yourself scalding a customer. So please always remember this: don't rush.

OK, that's the first one. Golden rule number two is: put things away. Kitchen staff, you can't leave things lying around, knives and so on, even if you think you're about to use them again. Just keep things out of harm's way. Housekeepers, when you're cleaning out the rooms, it's OK to leave the trolley in the corridor outside the room, but things like mops and buckets are a hazard if someone walks into them. So don't leave them lying around. The same goes for vacuum cleaners. Make sure you wind the cable back and store them safely in their cupboards.

If you're using some sort of cleaning agent in the bathrooms or whatever, make sure it's securely closed again, and put it back in the right place. Just put the things away.

Alright, now the third and final golden rule is: stop and check. So housekeepers, if you've just washed a bathroom floor, make sure it's dry enough so that someone won't slip and fall.

In the restaurant, maybe it's a bit quiet. Well, that doesn't mean you can just knock off for a cuppa. You need to remain alert – check for any spilt food and clear it up. Families with young kids especially – I'm sure you know what a mess they make.

Alright, well remember, there are quite a lot of accidents involving hotel staff in general. But I'm glad to say we've been extremely fortunate in that our safety record has been excellent. And that's how I'm sure we all want it to stay.

7c IT helpdesk
Track 11

Jackie: IT Services?

Stefan: Oh hello, is that, is that Jackie?

Jackie: Yes, it is.

Stefan: Oh hi Jackie, it's Stefan in Sales here.

Jackie: Hello Stefan.

Stefan: Hi there, thought I'd recognised your voice. Erm got a bit of a problem here, I'm afraid.

Jackie: Oh dear, well what's the trouble?

Stefan: Well, I've just had an email from my supervisor with an attachment that I'm supposed to print.

Jackie: And you can't?

Stefan: How did you guess?

Jackie: Well, have you checked if the printer's OK? The ink levels might be too low, that sort of thing.

Stefan: Yeah, well no, I mean the printer's fine, but the thing is it isn't letting me open the attachment at all.

Jackie: So what happens when you try?

Stefan: I get a pop-up message saying there is some error.

Jackie: OK, well is it all your emails, or just this one?

Stefan: I'm not sure. This is the only one I've opened today.

Jackie: OK, well look. What about going back into your inbox and trying another one? Anything with a similar attachment ideally, and let me know if that works.

Stefan: OK … just doing that now. No, that's OK, it's letting me download the attached document, no problem.

Jackie: Right.

Stefan: Well, what about, why don't I go back to the error message, cut and paste, and google it?

Jackie: Well, the thing is if you do that it'll suggest that you download something to fix the problem. But you won't be able to, I mean our system only allows someone with admin rights to download anything.

Stefan: Like you.

Jackie: Exactly. So the best thing to do is for you to forward me the email and I'll see what software you need and get that installed for you.

Stefan: Alright Jackie, I'll do that. Speak to you again soon.

Jackie: Cheers then. Bye.

8b Disability Discrimination Act
Track 12

Jermaine: Oh, alright Aziz. How was the DDA training yesterday?

Aziz: The Disability Discrimination Act stuff?

Jermaine: Yes, and that's a good start remembering what it stands for!

Aziz: Yeah.

Jermaine: So what did you find out from the training? The most important thing for you?

Aziz: Erm, well I'd say to treat all customers equally and never assume they have, or haven't got a disability.

Jermaine: Right.

Aziz: Well sometimes you can tell if someone has a disability, like if they're in a wheelchair, or if they have a guide dog. And often these people are totally capable of doing their shopping without extra help. But other people may have a disability you can't see, like a hearing impairment.

Jermaine: Exactly. Obviously a lot of people who do their shopping in our store have a condition covered under the Disability Discrimination Act. So, now you've attended this training, what will you change about the way you work to make sure their experience is a positive one?

Aziz: Well, some stuff I do anyway, like helping people at checkout pack their shopping, especially if they've got limited mobility or something. So I suppose it's just a matter of always thinking about what sort of help people might need. And it could be anything, couldn't it? I mean, like, some people can't reach up and get things off the top shelf.

Jermaine: OK. Well, look, Aziz, thanks very much for your comments. I'm really pleased the training was helpful.

Aziz: It really was. I learnt loads of new stuff.

8c Equal opportunities monitoring
Track 13

Gonzo: Alright Denise? How's it going?

Denise: Hi, Gonzo. How did you get on with that job application then?

Gonzo: Oh that one for South Hirton Council, you mean? Oh well, I had to fill in this form—

Denise: Application form?

Gonzo: No, well, yes, but I had to fill in another form. Yeah, but the thing is, the stuff they were asking on the form, a lot of it was, like, nothing to do with my suitability for the job. It was all about race and religion and stuff.

Denise: Well, they always do that kind of thing now, equal opportunities monitoring, they call it.

Gonzo: But why do they want to know what religion I am? I happen to be Christian, but I mean, why do they want to know that? That's my own private choice, innit?

Denise: So what did you do?

Gonzo: I thought, well, I'll just keep that to myself. They don't need to know – that was one of the options, anyway.

Denise: But you do know that it's just for statistical purposes, don't you? They don't use it to select people for the job. The people who look at your application form won't even see it.

Gonzo: I still think it's none of their business. Anyway the worst bit was the ethnic origin section.

Denise: Really? Well you just tick 'black' don't you? Just like I always choose 'Asian'.

Gonzo: No I can't really go for 'black'. 'Cos I'm mixed race, you see, my dad's Nigerian, and my mum's from Thailand. So I'm a mixture of black African and Asian.

Denise: Oh well, that's OK. They always have 'mixed race' as one of the options.

Gonzo: Well, yeah, they had that. But only 'black and white' or 'Asian and white'.

Denise: So what did you do?

Gonzo: I just went for 'other' in the end. And then you can write in your answer. So I put 'mixed Nigerian and Thai origin'.

Denise: Right.

Gonzo: But I tell you what though. I was tempted to just leave it blank.

Denise: Why?

Gonzo: Well, why should they care about ethnicity? I mean, if you're black, or white, or Bangladeshi, who cares? The whole point is, skin colour doesn't matter, does it?

Denise: Exactly, and I know it might not feel that way, but that's why you have to fill in this form, so that the council can check that there isn't any discrimination.

Gonzo: Yeah, well it's true the council's very multicultural. Got staff from all over the world. Let's hope I'll be one of them soon.

Denise: Yeah, fingers crossed!

9b Getting paid
Track 14

Sophie: Oh hello, Dariusz. Happy New Year to you.

Dariusz: Oh, thanks, and you too.

Sophie: Erm, can I just have a quick word?

Dariusz: Yes of course.

Sophie: Well, it's just that I don't seem to have received your pay claim form this month.

Dariusz: Sorry, what sort of form?

Sophie: Your pay claim form. Says when and how many hours you've worked. You fill that in, then submit it to me.

Dariusz: Oh right. But I only started last week. I've only worked three days.

Sophie: Yes, but the work you did was in December, and it's January now. You need to claim for last month's work on the first day of each new month.

Dariusz: So I can get paid, what, in a couple of days or so?

Sophie: No, we pay about one month in arrears.

Dariusz: One month in what, sorry? In arrears?

Sophie: That's it, yes, you get paid one month in arrears.

Dariusz: Right, sorry, I'm not exactly sure what that means.

Sophie: Well, basically, you get paid for the work you did in one month towards the end of the next month.

Dariusz: But I need to give you my pay claim at the start of the month?

Sophie: That's right. What happens then is that I check it, and if it's all OK, then I submit it to Payroll.

Dariusz: Payroll? Sorry, could you explain to me what Payroll does?

Sophie: Payroll – they're our people who do all the payments for all the staff. They process the payments by the 25th of the month.

Dariusz: Right. So, what you are saying is that I'll be paid for my work in December on about the 25th of January.

Sophie: That's it, yeah. So look, here's the form you need to complete, to erm, fill out.

Dariusz: Oh wow … looks a bit complicated.

Sophie: Oh it's not too bad, honestly. As it's your first one, why don't you fill it in the best you can, then bring it round to my office and I'll go through it with you. Make sure everything's right. How does that sound?

Dariusz: Oh, that's great, yeah, that'd be great, yeah thank you.

Track 15

Dariusz: Excuse me. Do you have a minute please?

Sophie: Yes, ah Dariusz, have you come with your claim form then?

Dariusz: Yes, I think I've done it all, well most of it, but if you wouldn't mind just checking it for me …

Sophie: Sure let's have a look. Now, ah Dariusz, you've written your name differently, you've put 'Darek'.

Dariusz: Yeah, Darek, it's short for Dariusz. Dariusz is, like, my official name, but Darek, my friends call me Darek.

Sophie: Oh right, so should I call you Darek then?

Dariusz: It's OK, I don't mind, both are alright. But is it wrong on the form?

Sophie: Well, yes, I think we need to keep with your official name really, because that's what it says on all our documents. So, I'll do it now. D-A-R-I-U-S, is that right?

Dariusz: Z

Sophie: So it's I-U-Z at the end?

Dariusz: No, I-U-S-Z, Dariusz, D-A-R-I-U-S-Z. In Polish, S-Z is 'shhh'.

Sophie: Ah right, I see. Like S-H in English then … So it's Dariusz not 'Darius' like I've been saying! OK. Back to the form. You need capitals for your surname, just makes it easier to read. So I'll change that.

Dariusz: Ah, so is that what 'block caps' means?

Sophie: That's right. Ah, and it looks like you've mixed up your National Insurance number and your employee number. They're in the wrong places.

Dariusz: Oh, I see.

Sophie: No problem, That's easy to fix. Now let's look at the hours worked. Err, OK you've worked from five till eleven thirty. You did have a break though?

Dariusz: Yeah, I'd been really busy and it was quite tiring, and I had to go to the loo.

Sophie: No no. That's fine. You do need to take your breaks. It's just that we don't pay you for them.

Dariusz: Oh right, I'm really sorry, I didn't want to, I mean, I thought that, well,

in my previous job we had breaks that were paid, so

Sophie: That's OK. It's an easy mistake to make. I'll just make that six hours worked instead of six and a half. Ah and here's another one!

Dariusz: Oh dear! What now?

Sophie: Don't worry, this one's in your favour. You've put down an hourly rate of £6.80 for both days, but the 31 December was New Year's Eve so the hourly rate is time and a half.

Dariusz: Time and a half?

Sophie: Yes, time and a half. It means an increase of 50 per cent on the normal rate, so it should be £10.20.

Dariusz: OK, that's great.

Sophie: So I'll just amend that. Er, yes, OK. So now I need you to sign this, then it can go to payroll to be processed. Oh, the only other thing is the box, you haven't ticked the box.

Dariusz: Can I see? *'I have worked as claimed above. I understand that making a false claim could lead to disciplinary action. Please tick to confirm the above information is correct.'* Oh, so is it a problem that I had the hours wrong? I'm not going to be in trouble am I?

Sophie: No of course not. We've corrected that, plus I know it was a misunderstanding. But you'll remember to take off breaks next time you claim, won't you?

Dariusz: Yes, of course, yeah, sorry about that. Anyway, thank you very much for your help.

Sophie: My pleasure, Dariusz. I hope it's been useful.

10a Phoning in sick
Track 16

Operator: Good morning. You're through to Thorntons Warehouse. How can I help you?

Hasan: Oh hello, could I speak to Sarah Howard, please?

Operator: Just a moment. Who's calling please?

Hasan: It's Hasan.

Operator: Oh hello Hasan. Just putting you through now.

Hasan: Thanks very much.

Sarah: Hello, Sarah Howard speaking.

Hasan: Oh hello. Sarah, this is Hasan speaking.

Sarah: Morning Hasan. What can I do for you today?

Hasan: Ah, well, it's just I'm not feeling very well today, so I'm afraid I won't be able to come in.

Sarah: Oh I'm sorry to hear that Hasan. What seems to be the trouble?

Hasan: Well, I think I've gone down with something, probably flu. I've got a splitting headache and I'm shivering. I just wanted to let you know as early as I could.

Sarah: Yes, thank you, I appreciate that. You're on the afternoon shift today, aren't you?

Hasan: Yes, 4 o'clock.

Sarah: OK, well I'm sure we can get someone to cover your shift.

Hasan: Do I need to get a doctor's note?

Sarah: Not unless you're going to be ill for five days!

Hasan: I hope not!

Sarah: Me too! What happens is you can self-certify for the first five days.

Hasan: Sorry? Self… self… I didn't catch that.

Sarah: Self-certify.

Hasan: Oh right, and er sorry, could you just explain what that means?

Sarah: Yes, well, in the UK, you can self-certify, so you can say that you don't consider yourself fit to work, you know, you don't think you're well enough and you can do that for the first five days of your illness. So, yeah, that's it really.

Hasan: OK, so can I do that when I come back?

Sarah: Yes, of course. No need to worry about it now! When you're back in, you need to fill in a form to confirm that you were off sick, and that just stays on our records.

Hasan: Ok I see. Thank you.

Sarah: So, yeah. Was there anything else?

Hasan: No, that's it. Thank you for your time.

Sarah: That's OK. And thank you for letting me know in good time. You have a good rest and get well soon.

Hasan: Thank you. Yes, I hope I'll be back soon. OK. Bye.

10b Dealing with customer complaints
Track 17

1   Thank you for calling Thomsons Building Supplies. Please leave a message after the beep. Thank you. [BEEP]

Yes, hello, yeah, hello there, Mr Sharma here, yeah, it's this order of ours for the steel rods to be delivered to the building site on Ship Road. We spoke about it yesterday. It's come, but I've checked and you've actually debited our account twice. Err, I don't know how that happened, but I'm not happy about paying for the same thing twice, so I'd like to know what you're going to do about it. Alright? So, if you could get in touch ASAP please. You should have my number: 77 44 22. Or send me an email. Bye.

2   Oh, er, morning, I thought you'd be open by now, it is nine o'clock already. Er, anyway this is Sam Harris. Er, well, there seems to have been some misunderstanding with the order. I wanted 20 plaster boards. That's what the order was for, that's what it says on your invoice. Not what you delivered us though unfortunately. You've brought us all sorts – plaster, timber, tiles mostly. Very kind of you. But not much use to us, as it's in the way. Speak soon. Oh, my number's 07737 298 107. Cheers now. Or my email, if you want it: harris@aecconstruction.co.uk. I'll just give you those again. My telephone number is 07737 298 107 or you can email on harris@aecconstruction.co.uk.

Track 18

Hello. Anna Hart speaking. I've just come back from holiday to find the timber we ordered. It's been delivered, but there's a problem because your delivery people, they just left it outside the house. Didn't cover it up or anything. Just left it there. So now, we've had a week of rain, and the wood's, well, basically ruined really, I'm afraid. We did explain we were going away, and you said you would get back to us with some possible delivery dates, but, well, we didn't actually hear back from you. Could you contact me, please? Email's best really: it's hart@nowmail.co.uk. Thanks.

11a What's the law?
Track 19

Interviewer: Right, I'm here with Manjula Ramasinghe, a lawyer who specialises in employment legislation.

Manjula: Thank you for inviting me in. I'm so pleased to have the opportunity to help people in understanding their employment rights.

Interviewer: Yes, well I'm sure our listeners out there will be very interested to hear what you've got to say. Let's start with pay. Can employers pay staff as much or as little as they want?

Manjula: As much, yes they can. But as little, absolutely not.

Interviewer: Now, this is the National Minimum Wage, isn't it – do employers have to stick to that?

Manjula: Well, in the past it was just a guideline, but it is now a legal obligation.

Interviewer: Right, so that applies to everyone?

Manjula: Well, yes it does, but you have to remember that it's a three-tier system.

Interviewer: How do you mean?

Manjula: Well, there's one rate for youngsters aged 17 or below, a slightly higher rate for people between 18 and 21, and then the adult rate.

Interviewer: Ah. On to other matters. Let's say someone has been offered and accepted a job, but not yet had a contract from the employer. Does that put them in a weak position?

Manjula: Well, yes and no. Obviously it would be advisable for both sides to get everything in writing—

Interviewer: Sure.

Manjula: but employers tend to take time to get all the paperwork done. The thing is, if you've started a job, and you haven't signed or even seen a contract, it's not the end of the world. You see, if an employer has given you a verbal offer of work with whatever salary or wage, then it is still—

Interviewer: legally binding?

Manjula: Exactly.

Interviewer: OK, so what about time off?

Manjula: Well, full-time workers are entitled to statutory holiday of 28 days a year.

Interviewer: Plus bank holidays?

Manjula: Ah, well not necessarily. There's a bit of a misconception about that. It's basically 28 days including bank holidays for most people, although some end up working on bank holidays. People need to check their own contracts for that, it all very much depends on the sector you're in.

Interviewer: Right, so if you work in an airport, say, it's likely that a bank holiday will be a normal working day, while, if you're, I don't know—

Manjula: A school teacher?

Interviewer: Exactly, then it won't. Is that right?

Manjula: That's just it. And another thing – the employer isn't obliged to pay a higher rate for that, like, an overtime rate for people who work on bank holidays.

Interviewer: But a lot do, though, don't they, like restaurants on New Year's Eve?

Manjula: Sure, well that's up to them.

Interviewer: It's easy to see why people get confused! And what about protecting people who work nights?

Manjula: Shift workers, you mean?

Interviewer: Exactly. Warehouses, hospitals, airports, bus depots – a lot of these places are staffed round the clock. I've heard there's a ban on them working nightshifts longer than eight hours, but is that actually enforced, do you think?

Manjula: Sorry, I have to correct you there. You're not quite right. You see, the law says they should work an *average* of not more than eight hours.

Interviewer: Oh, right, so if you do a nightshift of, say, nine hours one night, that's OK, your employer hasn't broken the law?

Manjula: No, that's fine, but then you'd do, say, maybe seven hours the next night, or something along those lines, so the average shift didn't go above eight hours.

Interviewer: Well Manjula, thank you. It's been fascinating. I'd love to ask you more, but we're just coming up to the 11 o'clock news, so we'll have to finish. Many thanks for coming in.

Manjula: It's been a pleasure.

12a Helping out
Track 20

1   A: Sorry, do you have a second?
    B: Yes, how can I help?
    A: I can't seem to find the biscuits.
    B: Right, well do you mean chocolate biscuits?
    A: No, you know, savoury biscuits, crackers, for having with cheese, not the chocolate ones. Could you just tell me where they are?
    B: Yeah, I'm here to help. You want aisle six.
    A: Aisle six?
    B: Yeah, you're quite close actually. You see where it says pasta, just there?
    A: Yeah.
    B: Well, just next to that basically.
    A: Oh yeah, right, I see. Thanks. Much appreciated.

2   A: Hello, can I help?
    B: Er, I was just wondering if you could just let me come and use the toilet quickly. Would that be OK?
    A: Well, the manager doesn't really, er… sorry, but I'm afraid the thing is, you know, it's supposed to be for the customers only. So the answer's going to have to be 'no' I'm afraid. Hey, excuse me!
    B: I'll only be a second!
    A: Some people!

From *English at Work* © CAMBRIDGE UNIVERSITY PRESS 2011   **PHOTOCOPIABLE**

3 A: Sorry, can I just ask you something?
B: Yes of course, what is it?
A: I'm here to visit my grandmother, Mrs Rose, Mrs Irene Rose.
B: Yes, that's fine. Visiting hours just started a minute ago, so you can go right in.
A: The thing is though, I don't actually know what ward she's in. Is this something you can help me with?
B: Right, I'll see what I can do. Sorry, won't be a minute, just checking for you. Yes, she's in ward twelve. So what you want to do is go down this corridor just here, take the lift to the second floor, and you'll see it right there.
A: That's very kind of you.

Audioscript 12b
Track 21
Helen: Did you see that article I emailed you?
Tim: The one about the green office? Yeah, I thought we could have a chat about it actually, see if we can make any changes that'd make our office a bit, well, you know, a bit greener. I've printed it off actually.
Helen: Not very green of you!
Tim: No, well, I have to say, I don't think we can do all of these things like in the article. Some of them, maybe. I mean, we're already quite frugal with our printing on the whole.
Helen: Printer can't do double-sided anyway.
Tim: That's right and no point buying a new printer – that'd be a waste.
Helen: Yeah, what about the cups though?
Tim: Oh, all those plastic cups we use and throw away? Stupid really!
Helen: Alright, so no more disposable cups then, yeah?
Tim: Alright, mugs it is then. Think we can just about manage that!
Helen: That's good! Oh, and it said something about all the electricity PCs use. Not sure we can afford to replace the PCs though, and get laptops. No, that'd be a false economy, wouldn't it, getting rid of them just so we'd have lower bills?
Tim: Mmm. But I think we could economise on the lights, I mean, we tend to leave them on all day, don't we? Cos the cleaner puts them on, I mean, it's probably dark when she comes in—
Helen: Yeah.
Tim: But do they have to stay on all day? Ditto with computers – we do have stuff on standby a lot. And I hear that on standby, a computer still uses as much power as an electric light.
Helen: All adds up then, doesn't it? Yeah, I think we could make some cuts there. Might have to nag each other a bit though, you know, reminding each other to turn stuff off.
Tim: Oh, you'll be good at that.
Helen: No comment. But I tell you what though, I think we're quite good with regulating the temperature. I mean, we don't overheat the place, do we?
Tim: No, no. And we've got no air conditioning.

Helen: Just open the window, don't we? If it's too hot.
Tim: Can't see the point of the plants though.
Helen: No, can't see a couple of little plants making much difference to the oxygen levels in our tiny little office, can you?
Tim: Just get in the way, they would. What about this, er, what do they call it now? Er telecommuting. Did that in my last job and loved it, just working at home in my pyjamas one day a week.
Helen: I can't see it doing us much good now though, can you? Or the environment, I mean, I walk to work, you cycle, so we've hardly got a heavy carbon footprint to worry about.
Tim: No, plus, to be honest, with the kids at home, I wouldn't get much done anyway. And I mean, cos it's just the two of us paying for this office, I'd rather come in, you know—
Helen: and get your money's worth from the rent on this place!
Tim: Exactly. OK, well we've got a few things we can start doing haven't we?
Helen: Yeah. Alright, well it feels like coffee time. Shall we pop out and buy those mugs?

13b Audioscript
Track 22
Right, well, it's been a funny old year really. More up-and-down than usual. But you always get a bit of that – it's just the nature of the work. We had a reasonable start to the year actually, with sales consistently going up. At least they did during the first quarter, but then they really dropped, and reached a low in May. Worst May on record for us this year actually. Things then got slightly better, only to fall in the third quarter. But then at the end of the year, we've been the busiest ever with sales going up, up and up, and reaching over 50,000 in December. So I'm quite optimistic about next year really.

Track 23
OK, well these precautionary measures are organised in schools, colleges, also some workplaces as well, er, including mine actually so that everyone knows what to do if there's …, if, you know, the worst happens. Last time we had one, there was a lady in a wheelchair, and she needed help getting out of the building. She works on the first floor right, but of course if you need to evacuate a building, you can't use the lift, you know, in case heat damages the workings, I think. Or, you know, in case smoke gets in.

Track 24
Receptionist: Heathfield Surgery. How can I help?
Mrs Edwards: Oh hello, this is Katy Edwards. I need to change an appointment.
Receptionist: Could you give me your date of birth?
Mrs Edwards: February the 14th, 1973.
Receptionist: Thanks. Right then.
Mrs Edwards: Well, I've got an appointment for Wednesday morning,

but I think I'm going to need to change it, because I've got someone coming.
Receptionist: OK. When would you like it for?
Mrs Edwards: Thursday would be best for me.
Receptionist: 11:30?
Mrs Edwards: Oh no, it'd need to be in the afternoon.
Receptionist: Nothing then, I'm afraid.
Mrs Edwards: Oh dear, well what about Tuesday then? I can do 11:30 then.
Receptionist: I'm afraid it's just afternoons on Tuesdays.
Mrs Edwards: Right. Erm, OK, well look we'll just have to leave it as it is.
Receptionist: OK, that's fine, so we'll see you then.

13c Evaluating a student's exam performance
Track 25
Examiner: OK Fatima, are you ready to start?
Fatima: Sorry, can I check something before we start?
Examiner: Yes of course.
Fatima: I imagine that I'm waiting, my, *my* company has ordered some stuff from *your* company, but I haven't had it yet. Is that right?
Examiner: That's exactly right. OK, so shall we start?
Fatima: OK. Ahem. Er good afternoon, this is Fatima Ismail here.
Examiner: Good afternoon, Ms Ismail. How can I help?
Fatima: Well, I'm calling from, er, Ismail Graphics Limited, and I wanted to speak to someone about a delivery.
Examiner: Well I should be able to help you with that.
Fatima: Oh good, well it's just that I ordered seven desktop computers and three printers. But I'm still waiting for them.
Examiner: Right, so what's the problem?
Fatima: Well that was over a month ago, and I'm still waiting for them. According our contract, you guarantee delivery within 28 days. So I'm concerned about what has happened.
Examiner: Oh I see, well I'll just check for you … Ah yes, I have your order here. It looks as if there's been a problem with the manufacturer, who are late in delivering to us. But we should be receiving the shipment next week.
Fatima: Next week? Oh dear, that's very late. I really need the order before then. I wonder, would you able to prioritise my delivery, so that I can take delivery as soon as possible.
Examiner: Fine, I'll do that then.
Fatima: Thank you. And do you know when it might be?
Examiner: Well, we can try and say Wednesday, but of course it all depends.
Fatima: OK, well that is appreciated. But, er, as I've been a very good customer of yours for some years now, I wonder if we could do something with price. Because you see, it's really rather inconvenient for me, this delay.
Examiner: I see. Well, I suppose we could take five per cent off, but that's the most we can do.

Audioscript

Fatima: OK, well that's appreciated. So I'll look forward to next week.

Examiner: Thank you Ms Ismail.

Fatima: Thank you. Bye.

Examiner: Thank you. That's the end of the roleplay. Are you happy with the outcome?

Fatima: Well, yes, absolutely. I think five per cent off a large order of expensive hardware, I mean yes that's a good reduction. I've probably saved a couple of hundred pounds. But you know what? I think maybe you were too quick to give me that discount! Yes, you see, in my country, we are very very tough negotiators!

14a Telephoning
Track 26

Ana: Good morning, you're through to Harrow Haircuts.

Mrs Brady: Oh hello, is that Ana speaking?

Ana: This is Ana, yes. How can I help?

Mrs Brady: Hello Ana, this is Mrs Brady speaking.

Ana: Morning Mrs Brady, how are you today?

Mrs Brady: Not bad thanks, yes. Er, any chance of an appointment this afternoon?

Ana: I'll just get the diary. Would you mind holding?

Mrs Brady: Not at all, that's fine.

Ana: I'm afraid we're fully booked this afternoon. But would tomorrow afternoon be OK?

Mrs Brady: What time?

Ana: How does 3:30 sound?

Mrs Brady: Oh, that's fine, yes, 3:30.

Ana: OK, well look forward to seeing you tomorrow then. Thanks for calling.

Mrs Brady: Right, OK then. Cheerio!

Track 27

Huda: Niceprice Online Supermarkets. You're through to Huda. Can I take your name please?

Alice: Oh hello, my name's Alice.

Huda: Morning Alice. Could I have your customer reference number please?

Alice: Yes, it's ACC512.

Huda: OK then, Alice. So, how can I help you today?

Alice: Well there's a bit of a problem with my order.

Huda: Right, so do you mean the wrong things were delivered?

Alice: No it's not that. I booked the delivery for tomorrow. But I have to go out.

Huda: I see, so you need to change the delivery time then?

Alice: Yes, that's right. I wasn't sure if I could do it on the Internet, so I thought I'd give you a ring.

Huda: Oh well, you can actually. It's quite easy to do online, just go to 'my account' and then click on 'change delivery details'. Just so you know for future reference.

Alice: OK, well perhaps I'll do that next time. It took ages to get through – I've been on hold for hours.

Huda: Yes, I'm afraid the switchboard has been very busy today. Anyway, when would you like to rearrange the delivery for?

Alice: Can we arrange it for Thursday about 4 o'clock?

Huda: Well, we can't guarantee the time, but we can give you a time slot of between two and five in the afternoon.

Alice: OK, well that's fine then.

Huda: Was there anything else I can help you with today?

Alice: No, that's fine, thank you very much for your help.

Huda: Well, you've been talking to Huda. Thank you very much for your call to Niceprice.

14b Service with a smile
Track 28
Conversation 1: Version A

Thabo: What do you want?

Customer: Erm, can I get one Hawaiian, please?

Thabo: What?

Customer: Could I have one Hawaiian please?

Thabo: Is that all you're going to buy?

Customer: Just the pizza, please.

Thabo: Sit down and wait.

Customer: OK, do you know roughly how long it'll be?

Thabo: Look, I'll do it as quick as I can. Alright?

Customer: OK, fine, I'll sit here and wait.

Track 29
Conversation 1: Version B

Thabo: Hello madam, what would you like?

Customer: Erm, can I get one Hawaiian, please?

Thabo: I'm sorry. What was that?

Customer: Could I have one Hawaiian please?

Thabo: Certainly, would you like anything else with that?

Customer: Just the pizza, please.

Thabo: OK, if you'd like to take a seat, I'll give you a shout when it's ready.

Customer: OK, do you know roughly how long it'll be?

Thabo: Shouldn't be too long. I'll do it as quick as I can for you, madam.

Customer: OK, fine, I'll sit here and wait.

Track 30
Conversation 2: Version A

Customer: Oh hello, does this go to Station Road?

Adam: Yes.

Customer: Oh good. One then, please.

Adam: Single or return?

Customer: Sorry?

Adam: Single or return?

Customer: Oh, I see, well, yes. Just a single then.

Adam: A pound.

Customer: Right, here's a tenner.

Adam: I don't want that. I want a pound.

Customer: Oh, let's see what I've got. Oh yes, here you are.

Adam: Take your ticket.

Track 31
Conversation 2: Version B

Customer: Oh hello, does this go to Station Road?

Adam: It does, yes. Takes about 15 minutes.

Customer: Oh good. One then, please.

Adam: OK, and is that a single or return?

Customer: Sorry?

Adam: Just one way, or are you coming back?

Customer: Oh, I see, well, yes. Just a single, then.

Adam: That's a pound then, please.

Customer: Right, here's a tenner.

Adam: No change I'm afraid. Do you have anything smaller?

Customer: Oh, let's see what I've got. Oh yes, here you are.

Adam: Thanks. Don't forget your ticket.

Track 32

Customer: You're not closing yet, are you?

Shop assistant: Well, we do actually close at 8:30, so I'm afraid you're a bit late.

Customer: Oh, please, I just want a bottle of milk.

Shop assistant: I'm really sorry, I've already shut down the till, so I can't accept any more sales today.

Customer: But I'm a regular customer. I come here every day.

Shop assistant: I know, I'm really sorry. But the grocer's next door stays open till 10. You'll be able to get some there.

15c Checking details
Track 33

Student 1: OK, so we're going to this training thing, yeah, and we just need to check that we've got all the right details.

Student 2: Yeah, we don't want to all go off to different places.

Student 3: Or on different dates!

Students 1 and 4: Yeah!

Student 1: Right, so the training's in November, isn't it? That's what it said on the website.

Student 4: November, yeah.

Student 3: The 22nd, yes. I checked on the phone actually, listened to a long recorded message.

Student 2: Hang on, are you sure it's November the 22nd, not October? It's just that my information says 22/10, that's October isn't it? October's the 10th month right?

Student 3: Erm, yeah, that's right. Because if December's the 12th, being the last, then November's the 11th and October's the 10th.

Student 2: OK, so there's a mix-up here isn't there? I mean we can't all be right.

Student 1: Well, the rest of us think it's November so I'd assume the three of us are right.

Student 2: OK, so it's definitely not October. I'll just cross that out.

Student 3: Yeah, so we're all going to the training in November. You can go in October if you want, but I think you'll be on your own!

Student 2: No, no, it's OK, I'll come with you in November! November the 22nd. Can I just double-check that? It was the 22nd, wasn't it?

Student 4: Yeah, the 22nd, yes. Well, we just saved you a wasted trip there, so I think you owe us one!

Student 2: Saved me some money as well, I should think. £37.50 to get there by train!

Student 3: Is that definitely right? Cos I think it'd be more than that, I mean if you're going there and back …